I Left A Mess
In There

By

RASHAD "SHADCORE" HARRELL

I Left A Mess In There is a work of nonfiction.

Copyright ©2025 Rashad Harrell
St. Petersburg, FL

All rights reserved.

Published by Rashad Harrell

ISBN Paperback: 979-8-9933672-0-0
ISBN Hardcover: 978-8-9933672-2-4
ISBN eBook: 978-8-9933672-1-7
ISBN Audio Book: 978-8-9933672-3-1

Printed in the United States of America

Book Cover design by Troy Cedeño

Typesetting by Marlon McCaulsky

Edited by Autumn Harrell

Also by Rashad "Shadcore" Harrell

I WANNA RAP RIGHT NOW!

To anyone who has ever had the audacity to dream BIG dreams!

"I rap. A lot. And I'm pretty good at it. The end." -
SHADCORE

*To anyone who has ever had the audacity to dream
BIG dreams!*

"I rap. A lot. And I'm pretty good at it. The end." -
SHADCORE

CONTENTS

FOREWORD

Working with Shadcore was a great experience, because not only was he professional and personable, but his music is fire. When I first spoke to him and he told me the joint I was going to be on was titled "AUX-Tales", A-U-X tales, I knew then I was gonna luv it. The funny thing about that song is I loved the final piece so much, I told Shad, "I wished I had written that one for myself." A friend of mine goes on and on about that piece til this day! It's his favorite.

Shadcore has a real genuine love for Hip-Hop, and that's something I really respect about him. He's the type of artist that goes beyond the obvious or the "safe" zones when it comes to his art. I appreciate the way he provides a unique perspective in his music, something that he continues to do on his new album, as well as his book; both of which are titled *I Left A Mess In There*. Like I said, Shadcore is different. Not too many artists couple entire books along with their albums. That's definitely a boss move on his part.

When you read and experience *I Left A Mess In There*, you will be taken on a journey that truly defines the title. You'll understand that Shadcore is an artist that will definitely leave his mark in history. I can appreciate that, because I'm a firm believer in caring about the legacy you leave behind, and I believe Shadcore cares a lot about his.

I'd like to thank Shadcore for letting me deliver this foreword to his brand new masterpiece, *I Left A Mess In There*. Shadcore, tell your story, bruh.

Ruben "Big Rube" Bailey
August 2025

by RASHAD "SHADCORE" HARRELL

INTRODUCTION

I wanted to do something great and uncommon when I decided to write this book. There are a couple things that I know for sure. I was born to rap and I was born to write! This was established long before I discovered my passion for both. God gave me these gifts as a tiny seed. It doesn't matter if it's in the form of a song, book, movie script or poem, I absolutely love creative writing and telling inspirational stories. It's been about four years since I released my last album. During the process of making this album, I began to realize just how special the music felt and sounded to me. I noticed, *Everything that you need is already on the inside of you!* Your potential for greatness was embedded in you upon conception. God placed it there. Just as a tiny seed has the growth potential to become a sky-piercing tree, such is true for your physical and your spiritual makeup. You don't search for greatness. Greatness lives *in* you! Strive to be all that you were designed to be. Unfortunately, many people live far below their potential. Sure, life is full of its challenges, difficulties and various circumstances, but the mere existence and presence of these things in our lives doesn't define who we are - however, how we respond to them does.

I fell in love with hip-hop music around the age of 9 when my older cousin, Derek Lee, gave me a cassette tape with a mix that included Run-D.M.C., LL Cool J., The Fat Boys, UTFO, Whodini and The Beastie Boys. Even though I really liked the music my parents played around the house, like Stevie Wonder, Michael Jackson, and Marvin Gaye, hip-hop spoke to me in a completely different and energetic kind of way. The hard-hitting drums, the rhythmic flows and the way the rappers put their words together was like one big sugar rush and, instantly, I was addicted. It wouldn't be long before I found myself attempting to do the very thing that I heard my hip-hop heroes doing. I got pretty good at it over time, too.

I remember telling my 5ᵗʰ grade teacher that I wanted to be a rapper when I grew up and the perplexed look on Mrs. Baker's face when I told her that. The more I tried, the better I got. I wrote every day, non-stop. I improved on my craft verse by verse, until I eventually began to show my friends and family some of my rhymes. I entered talent shows, performed in school lunch rap battles and, by the time I became a senior, my classmates were calling me by my new stage name – SHADCORE.

I rediscovered that same joy and passion I had as a kid when I was creating this album. It's not like I ever fully lost the passion but, if I'm being honest, I struggled with feelings of discontentment and discouragement for years. I always believed that I'd be doing music full-time. To feed my family and earn a decent living off the gift God gave me is my true desire. "I'm just as good as the next guy", I often reasoned. As we all know, things don't always turn out as planned, so after working three decades of regular jobs, doubt began to rear its ugly face. Am I really cut out for this? Maybe I'm not meant to do this on a full-time basis. Is it ever going to happen for me? These feelings can stifle the creative process altogether.

Now don't get me wrong; I have enjoyed a wonderful life. I've been married to a remarkable woman for over 25 years, and we share three amazingly gifted children together, as well as a beautiful little granddaughter. I also gained a wonderful daughter-in-love. God has shined his light on me, and I am grateful for His favor and His love. There have been some valleys along the way, though. Losing my father in 2014 to a massive heart attack was devastating. I really hoped that my dream would have come into fruition during his lifetime because he was my hero and the one who introduced music to me in the first place. Despite all the life that has occurred since my senior year in high school, one thing that never wavered was my love for rapping.

In my close to 50 years of living, I've watched music evolve and the way we consume it. There have been several mediums over the last four decades in how music has been presented to the consumer. I was there to witness the transition from vinyl to cassette, cassette to CD, CD to MP3 and lastly, MP3 to streaming. With each transition I was a little reluctant to jump on board. As a kid, I remember pulling the sleeves out of my daddy's vinyl records and reading the liner notes. On many occasions the artist would include the lyrics to the songs so, for me, it was an added bonus to read the words while listening to the music.

I particularly enjoyed when Prince would release an album because he was very creative in the style in which the words were printed. For example, the word "I" would be replaced with the image of an eye, instead. He'd also use the letter "U" in place of the word "you" and a heart symbol for the word "love". I was fascinated with that level of creativity and, even at the age of 10, I understood that Prince was setting himself apart from everyone else, just off of his lyric presentation alone.

Nevertheless, vinyl would ultimately be replaced, as the preferred medium, by the cassette tape. I had no choice but to get on board and eventually I grew to love listening to tapes. I amassed a huge collection over time, and would pop them into my Sony Walkman, one after the other. I'd close my eyes and escape to wherever that artist was taking me at that moment. Next thing you know, the compact disc entered the room and threw the cassette in an inescapable chokehold. CDs were more expensive than tapes, but the freedom they gave you to instantly skip from track to track was undeniably enticing. Plus, the hiss from playing cassettes was removed for more clarity with the invention of the compact disc.

I could remember thinking to myself "this is as good as it's gonna get." I didn't think there were any new ways to "play music" after the CD but, boy, was I wrong! The MP3 changed the game entirely. No longer did you have to lug around those colossal-sized 50 CD-carrying booklets. Now, literally, thousands of songs could fit right into your pocket with the invention of the iPod. I still enjoyed my CDS, though, so I went kicking and screaming into this non-physical copy world. I liked having something tangible in my hand that I could actually feel and touch. I held on for as long as I could, but I gave in, eventually.

I remember both the first and the last CD that I purchased. Guy's *The Future* was the first, back in 1992 and Bruno Mars' *24K Magic* was the last in 2016. Here's the irony of those two albums: in '92, Guy had their sights on the future, pushing the New Jack Swing genre forward, while in 2016 Bruno Mars opted to pay homage to that same New Jack Swing era! It was a retro throwback that earned

Bruno a grammy nod for Album of The Year. As I'm writing this, it really just hit me- the more things change the more they stay the same! Music is cyclical, much like a revolving door.

While there is an obvious convenience to having unlimited music at your fingertips, there is also the threat of oversaturation. How do we learn to sit with and truly appreciate a body of work when there are so many choices to choose from? It's so easy, nowadays, for something special to get overlooked, because you never really soaked it in due to option-overload. For just $9.99 a month, every song that ever existed is at your disposal.

However, what inevitably happens, as a result of this luxury, is a certain devaluation of the music and the art. See, what I miss about the physical copy is the experience of actually going outside to shop for the music. I miss the anticipation of release day, when you would walk inside the record store and head straight to the "rap/hip-hop" section to hold that cellophane-wrapped CD in your hands. I couldn't wait to bite into that plastic and rip it off, as I hopped in my whip, eager to insert that disc in and listen to that first track! It was almost communal when a Wu-Tang or an OutKast would drop, as you stood in the checkout line, amongst other fans, all clutching the same CD in your hands.

I also miss the time spent actually listening to and studying an album in its entirety. Back then you went on a journey with the artist. Instead of just skipping to their hit single, you took your time with each song, allowing the artist to slowly reveal themselves. That's the beauty of a great body of work. It's a plethora of moods, feelings and emotions, all designed to connect with the listener on a deeper level with the art that's being presented.

The previous sentence is the whole motivation behind writing this book. *I Left a Mess in There* is more than just another album. It's an emphatic imprint, intended to be enjoyed as a full body of work. I want to give you those same feelings I felt when I stood in those long lines at Circuit City, Best Buy or the local mom and pop shop, anticipating pressing "play" the first moment I got. The excitement of hearing incredible bars from my favorite emcees, over hard-hitting beats, is what I want to create for you.

With attention spans seemingly decreasing by the minute, this time around required an unconventional approach. For the music to truly be appreciated, as it should, I needed to go the extra mile on this project because it truly is that special.

I had to combine those two aforementioned things that I know for sure about myself together with one another. I was born to rap and to write so why not write a book about the process of making an incredible album? Although vinyl still exists (it's making quite a comeback, actually), I know this album will mostly be listened to on digital platforms, but the book could satisfy that missing tangible component.

I'll never forget what my Godmother and First Lady of our church, Jean Freshler, told me when I went "live" with my last album on Facebook. I played each song, one by one, and gave a quick backstory on how each song came to be. She commented on how much she enjoyed listening to the process and how it made her feel that much more connected to the music. Her words stuck with me and they came to my remembrance as I was creating this album.

To write an entire book seemed like a lofty goal, which is the very reason I pursued it. Our dreams should scare us a little. If they don't then perhaps they aren't big enough. I knew I needed supernatural favor from God to pull this off, especially with how busy my day-to-day schedule is.

For the next 15 chapters you will get a detailed behind-the-curtain look at how each song was created and the inspiration behind them. This album is an exhilarating roller coaster ride that will make you think, laugh, bob your head and even cry a tear or two. This book is the exclamation point that the album deserves. Get lost in it. Search for the parallels and correlations in your own life as you read along. My purpose in all of this is to inspire. Thank you for reliving this journey with me. As my passenger in the cockpit, you have been granted access into my psyche and, prayerfully, by arrival you'll know exactly what it means to "leave a mess in there". Strap in!

CHAPTER 1:
BE YOU
(I'm That Boy!)

S et the tone. I believe that's what every first song on an album is supposed to do. Come out swinging, so to speak, and leave that proverbial first impression. Sometimes a song just happens to become the album opener and other times you write a song, intentionally, to set things off. I wrote "I'm That Boy!" specifically, to be a tone-setter. When I first heard the instrumental, I said to myself "This is the kinda beat where you make an introduction to the world!"

The music took me back to a pivotal time in my life, circa the early 90's, when I was a member of my first rap group, BRUTAL FUNK. The name BRUTAL is an acronym for *Bringing Rap Up To Another Level.* You're going to find out that I have a strong fetish and a bit of a knack for creating acronyms as you read along.

The original members were JayFunk, Double R and myself. JayFunk and I met in high school and we quickly became friends, upon discovering our mutual love for the rapper Rakim. When he heard me rhyme for the first time, he even said that I reminded him of Rakim! JayFunk told me he made beats and that his younger brother, Double R, could sing. We arranged a meet-up at their house, just to see what each other could do. I was blown away at how dope JayFunk's beats were and how much his little brother sounded like a young Michael Jackson! When Double R heard me rap, he told his brother "he *does* sound like Rakim!" We knew at that moment we wanted to form a group so that's exactly what we did.

We needed to come up with a name to call ourselves, so we began brainstorming and throwing out ideas. I went home, grabbed my notebook, and started jotting down different words. I knew I wanted our name to stand out from everyone else. Back then, originality was paramount. I was really into the hard, aggressive emcees of that era like Chuck D., Ice Cube, Redman and EPMD., to name a few. I wanted our name to have an edge to it, much like those rappers had, and even as a 16-year-old kid, I wanted our name to be an acronym that was unique. The word "brutal" came to mind and it just stuck out amongst all the other words on the paper. After about an hour of trying to come up with a suitable acronym, it's almost as if the sky parted and God, himself, came into my bedroom and whispered, "bringing rap up to another level.".

I thought to myself, "this is it" but I wasn't sure how JayFunk and Double R would feel about it. I called them up and when I told them my idea, they both said "Shad, that's it!"

I was so excited! We immediately went to work, making beats and writing songs. However, our equipment at the time was very limited so JayFunk and I decided to put our funds together to purchase a beat machine for the group. I still remember the name of it-The BOSS Dr. Rhythm 550! We instantly fell in love with this tiny machine that produced these huge sounds.

Being a hip-hop head, especially one from the South, my favorite sound that came out of that machine was the 808 kick drum. I felt a rush every time one of us pressed that button. It sounded "brutal" and ultimately it became a part of our signature sound, a term we eventually coined "Brutal Funk." The 808, coupled with long sustained low end bass notes was our go-to formula. It seemed to compliment my baritone voice perfectly.

When I heard the beat for "I'm That Boy!" it instantly transported me back to JayFunk and Double R's den, a place that we called the "Brutal Lab." We literally spent hours upon hours in that hot, small room that was once a garage-turned-living space. We didn't know it at the time, but we were essentially becoming outliers. The ten thousand hours of perfecting our craft was met well before we even entered the 21st century!

Eventually our group grew larger. We added a young incredibly talented musician named Steve, who I nicknamed Yamajesteve before he settled with Black Speed, and two more dynamic emcees, D. A. and King Spry. We started doing shows and quickly made a name for ourselves in our hometown of St. Petersburg, Florida. I absolutely loved sharing the mic with my brothers D.A. and King. We pushed one another to be the best we could possibly be.

I had a reputation back then, and still do to this day, of completing my verse before anyone else on a group track. I do that because I believe it's my job to "set the tone". Not to sound cocky, but I know what I bring to the table and my collaborators know it too. I'm that boy! The one who will provide wit, lyricism, confidence and a straight up wow-factor to any project I touch. With over 35 years of experience, I have developed a standard that demands anyone working with me to raise the bar. It's who I am. All I know is bars and creativity. I don't know how to "dumb it down" because I was trained by artists like Rakim, Big Daddy Kane, KRS-One and Chuck D. to have something to say in a witty way.

"I'm That Boy!" was written as a reminder, to myself, that I am indeed that dude. The one that used to have my boys making the "stank face" when they heard me spit. The beat took me right there. It sounded like something JayFunk or Black Speed would've made. The familiarity was uncanny.

The funny thing is I have never actually met the producer in person. I received the instrumental via email. His producer name is Ankor Beats. I'm not even sure how he got my email, but I'm glad he did. Ankor Beats is just one of three producers on the album who I'll refer to as the "cold email producers."

The 808s hit so hard on this song, so I had to match their energy. I wanted the listener to know I meant business on this record. I believe there is an art to matching the right words and subject matter with the right music. The two should complement one another and not compete against. If done correctly, it will sound like audible holy matrimony.

I titled this chapter "Be You" because that's precisely what I had to do over this beat. I had to be Shadcore. What that means is I had to do what I'm known for - BEATING UP BEATS! I take it as a personal challenge, when presented with a bangin' beat, to not let it outshine me. At the end of the day, I can't have anyone saying "well, I like the beat but…" If the music wows whoever hears it, then best believe my rhymes will too.

It requires commitment and dedication to reach that level, though. It doesn't just happen overnight. You have to get into your own "brutal lab" and put that work in. Hone your craft. You can't say "I'm That Boy" if you haven't established that reputation yet.

I open the first verse up with a hidden gun reference, which I quickly dispel by saying "my wife will even tell you I'm just one big teddy bear." In other words, I'm saying that's not really me. Even though a lot of rappers glamorize guns and street life in their music, that's not who Shadcore is. It never has been and it never will be. I'm perfectly ok with shooting rapid fire in the form of bars and not bullets. It would be totally off brand for me to glorify gun use on any record.

You have to be comfortable with being who you are. I don't use profanity in my music either. I made that choice when I first started rapping and I've stuck with it ever since. I stood out because of it. It's usually one of the first things people notice when they hear me rhyme. I can remember on several occasions when folks would say things like "you probably would have *been* signed by now if you cussed in your songs." They were probably right but that would not have been me. I liked standing out from everyone else, so that never bothered me. My dad told me at a very young age that a man curses because he lacks the vocabulary to express himself. Those words stuck with me and carried me as a writer for nearly 40 years. In fact, every single time I write a new rhyme I try to include a word that I haven't used in a song before. This exercise keeps the writing process fun and exciting for me. I welcome the challenge.

One of my favorite things about working on an album is coming up with the title for it. You usually discover that along the way, or at least that's been my experience in the past. I was about 3 or 4 songs in before I even realized I was in the midst of making a new album. What I mean by that is there are times when you record a song or two just because you love the art and you have to scratch that creative itch. Your intentions may not be to put out a full project, but this keeps the juices flowing. I couldn't deny how cohesive the songs I had recorded felt and that's when it dawned on me that I was actually making a new Shadcore album.

We have a family friend named Dominique and she once complimented me on how creative my album titles were. She loved *Oh My Shad!* and *AUX Tales.* I'm really big on coming up with conversation-starters and making statements. As I was trying to come up with a title for this album, I had Dominique's voice in the back of my head and I'd often think "would Dominique like this title?"

One day I was listening to *"I'm That Boy!"* and there was a line on the first verse that just smacked me right in the face. I said *"I made sure the dude that came behind me was well aware, before he entered the booth, that I left a mess in there!"* Just like JayFunk and Double R said when I came up with the group name BRUTAL, I said, "Shad, that's it!" I Left a Mess In There! What a statement! Images for the album artwork started racing through my mind. I saw myself on the cover, walking away from a burning recording studio, much like the stereotypical Hollywood shot of the hero walking away, totally unfazed by the catastrophic explosion right behind him! I felt ignited and ready to go that much harder, now that I knew the official album title. It's crazy how these things can reveal themselves when you least expect them to.

The first person I shared the title with was my friend, Justin Finity. Justin provides the ad libs for this track. We used to work at the same job during the making of this song. I asked him if he'd be down to do some ad libs for a new song I was working on because I loved his energy. I wanted it to feel like Chuck D. and Flava Flav all over again and Justin was the perfect candidate to bring Flav's "Yeah Boyeeee!!" energy to the song. He's a great rapper, himself, as you will find out on his song, *Carnage*, that features a verse from yours truly. I had been on sort of a hiatus when Justin reached out to me to see if I'd be interested in writing a guest verse for his song. He woke up the beast in me when we did that record together so it was only right that he be the first voice you hear on my new album. Justin helped me remember that I am that boy!

The same excitement JayFunk and Double R felt when they first heard me rap is what I wanted the listener to experience when I wrote this song. I had my brothers in mind the entire time. I wanted D.A. and King to say "boy, you still got it!" I can't wait to get all of their takes once they've heard it. If they say "Shad, that's it" then I know for sure that I took care of business.

CHAPTER 2:
Keep It Movin'
(We Got Motion)

I t took 47 years for me to take my first cruise and only 6 months afterwards to take my second one. I couldn't believe I had waited so long to treat myself to such an incredible expedition. The excitement and entertainment on board was intoxicating (figuratively, of course). The calmness of the sea was extremely tranquil. You can't even begin to appreciate how vast the ocean is until you're sailing atop its waters and you realize there isn't a speck of land in sight. Getting to meet the local Bahamians and cracking jokes with the Mayan tour guide in Cozumel were interactions that I never knew I needed. Nevertheless, they were blessed moments in my life.

I knew a couple of months prior to embarking on my second cruise that I was going to write this book, but it wasn't until the fifth day on board that I actually decided to pick up the pen and let loose. I figured what better atmosphere to unlock my thoughts and let my ideas run free than this amazing scenery that God so wonderfully created! What's interesting is I came up with the song in between the first and the second cruise. On one hand I had the benefit and luxury of having taken my debut cruise to the Bahamas to draw firsthand experience from to help aid me in writing the song. On the other hand, I had the anticipation of the upcoming second cruise to Cozumel, Mexico to guide me to the completion of the song.

I originally wrote and recorded an entirely different song to the beat a year prior to making the album version. I was never one hundred percent satisfied with the original version though. The first draft was called "Mushmouth". I was basically telling the audience that I was not like a lot of these mumble rappers that you hear today. I wanted the listener to know that I prided myself on articulating every syllable that I uttered. The problem was it really was just an album-filler and one thing I never wanted to do was throw a song on a project just to take up space. I tried several times to talk myself into leaving the song as is. "But the beat is so dope," I said to myself. "Boy, look how you're riding the track," I frequently reasoned. However, none of those thoughts were louder than "Shad, you know you can do better!"

One day I looked at my potential tracklist and "Mushmouth" just stood out like a sore thumb. Every other song up until that point had some weight and substance to it except this one. So, I decided to scrap the original idea, but I knew better than to throw the baby out with the bathwater. I got rid of the lyrics and I kept the beat. I chose to go in a brand new direction this time around. I had to search through my email so I could find the instrumental track to write to.

I spend a lot of time in the car en route to both of my jobs so I figured this would be the perfect opportunity to put the beat on repeat and create something entirely new. As I listened to the music with a fresh set of ears, I couldn't help but notice how "wavy" the composition sounded. The bassline was so groovy. The piano melody was simple, yet catchy. I loved the female vocal sample in the intro, although I still can't quite make out exactly what she is saying. What's important is that it sounds and it feels right. That's what music boils down to – how does it sound and how does it make me feel? The waviness of the production reminded me of being on a cruise ship and just like that a new concept was born - "We Got Motion!"

I was excited when the idea came because I knew once I had a concept I liked, the lyrics would flow effortlessly. Now remember I had already thrown out the original lyrics, but for the song to "feel" brand new to me I also had to do away with the original flow and cadence. I started with the hook first. I wanted to surf over the track this time around! It didn't take long before I found a new pocket to flow in. Usually it's customary for the flow and cadence of the hook to differ from that of the verse, but I liked how I was flowing on the hook so much that I chose to keep that same flow for the verses as well. I also thought it would be a fun challenge to keep the rhyming sound the same throughout the entire song. As an artist, I find it necessary to stretch yourself beyond your own expectations.

Never have I recorded a song (which means I paid someone my hard-earned money), only to later record a whole new song to the same beat and have to pay again. That's too much like double work and I hate double work with a passion. I had to get it right this time. I felt good about the concept along with the new flow that I came up with and the overall direction of the song, but I needed to avoid the mistake I made the first time, which was making a "weightless" song.

I love metaphors and similes so I began to focus on the title of the song "We Got Motion." "What does that mean, exactly?" I pondered. Well motion, obviously, means things are constantly moving and not sitting idle. This realization was the first piece of the puzzle that solidified my decision to sail a different route with the beat. Now I had the right tools in my toolbox to build a masterpiece.

Just like waves in the sea, we should also be in constant motion. Whether that's physical motion or motion in the form of our thoughts and ideas, it's imperative that we "keep it moving." Everything in life revolves around motion. Time doesn't stand still. The earth is constantly spinning. What good is your automobile if it isn't moving?

I'm reminded of the excursion my wife and I went on the day before I began to pen this book. We rode ATVs through the Mexican jungle. What made that excursion so exhilarating was the fact that we indeed had motion. Riding those high-powered vehicles over the rocky asphalt was an experience neither one of us will soon forget. My point is it requires movement. An idle life is a rather boring life. Find an activity that you love, or at least like, and then engage. So many people have zero motion or anything interesting going on in their lives and, unfortunately, misery loves company. Avoid those types at all costs. Don't sit on the sidelines, spectating and complaining. Get in the game and make a play!

I purposely created two different scenarios for the verses. In the first verse I wanted to paint a picture of some friends on a yacht, celebrating their homeboy's huge job promotion. The reason that was important to me is because it showcases brotherhood and true friendship, which doesn't include jealousy or envy. We can genuinely be happy for one another when we receive these wins. Shining a light on your brother in no way diminishes your own. If you want to be a winner, then hang around other winners! Be careful not to fall into that negative way of thinking, "why him or her and not me?" In fact your thought process should be "if God did it for them then He'll surely do it for me," because He is not a respecter of persons.

On the second verse my focus was on spending quality time cruising the seas with my beautiful wife. She is my muse for a large portion of my material as you'll often find throughout this book. Together we've had motion for more than 25 years and we're still finding new ways to maintain that motion. I've penned so many songs about her during that time, yet I'm still discovering a variety of ways to express my love for her through music. Every lyric in that second verse is true and that's what makes it so special. I love the way her face lights up when she hears me rapping about her.

I also liked the idea of creating a cruise anthem song. Let's face it, people enjoy taking cruises. I figured, as far as I know, there weren't any official songs related to "cruise life" so why not make one of your own? If you add it to your playlist the next time you decide to go cruising, then it's safe to say my mission was accomplished.

This song was also produced by Ankor Beats, the producer behind "I'm That Boy!" There are some very good producers out there. I opened myself up on this album to work with different people who were outside of my usual network. This was a new approach for me because I am used to being in the same room, working with and right next to the producer. It almost always starts out as a friendship that morphs into a producer/artist relationship. However, on *I Left a Mess in There* 85% of the production was handled by producers who I have never met in person. I haven't even had an audible conversation with them before. These are the cold email producers I referred to in the first chapter.

The message would usually read as follows: "If you rock with my beats, DM me!" I would receive these emails from various producers at least three times a week. I usually would ignore them and keep it moving, speaking of motion. For whatever reason, one day I decided to click the link in one of those emails to check the beat out. I was pleasantly surprised at the level of quality in the production and how the beat made me feel. I began digging through old emails from not only this producer but others to see if there were some potential gems that I was missing out on. This became my approach to amass production for the album. Unconventional? Maybe, but something new and exciting, nevertheless. This was just another way to keep the motion of my artistry alive by allowing myself to try something new.

CHAPTER 3:
Nah You Ain't Done
(NYAD)

Inspiration is a funny thing because it can come in ways and forms that you least expect. I couldn't have anticipated the way a certain movie I watched one weekend would move me to write perhaps the album's most inspirational song. The parallels to my experience as a songwriter, in a relentless pursuit to achieve my dream, were undeniable when I learned the story of Diana Nyad in the movie titled *Nyad*.

Ms. Nyad is a long-distance swimmer who gained national attention in 1975 (the same year I was born) when she swam 28 miles in record time around the city of Manhattan. Four years later she achieved an even more remarkable feat when she swam 102 miles from Bimini, Bahamas to Juno Beach, Florida! Now, of course, when Diana accomplished these victories, she was in her 20s. It reminded me of a few proud moments in my own life as a rapper that I was able to achieve in my 20s.

In 2001 I entered a jingle-writing competition, where the grand prize was a brand-new car! The contestants were tasked with creating a one-minute song about the new Kia Rio that was making its debut that year. Each participant was asked to include the same five features about the vehicle and whoever delivered the most creative take would drive home in a brand-spanking-new car. After narrowing the competition down to 20 finalists, I ultimately walked away (or should I say drove away) the victor!

In 2005 and 2006 I was a Top 5 finalist in a freestyle rap competition held by VH-1. The name of the contest was Freestyle59, in which unsigned artists submitted a fifty-nine second video of them performing their best freestyle rap. VH-1 selected the top 25 submissions in the country, then a panel of 5 celebrity judges, which included Public Enemy's front man Chuck D., narrowed it down to the best five. The Top 5 were flown to the VH-1 studios in Times Square New York and given the opportunity to record a new nationally televised video. Viewers cast their votes online to determine the winner. I was the runner-up in 2005 and I took third place in 2006.

It's worth noting that with the car and with VH-1, I was confident that I would win. You must believe in yourself long before you attempt to do something great. Just as Diana Nyad would have never set foot in the ocean if she didn't think her goal was possible. Put in the work and trust the process. Nyad trained vigorously to complete those swims, perfecting her craft through commitment and preparation. I, too, spent plenty of hours, prior to those contests, writing in my bedroom, school, lunch breaks or wherever I could get my hands on a pen and pad, striving to be better than I was the day before. One does not swim from the Bahamas to Florida, nor write jingles to win cars, without a considerable amount of practice.

This story gets even sweeter, and this is what truly inspired me to write "NYAD" otherwise known as "Nah, You Ain't Done." (I told y'all I love my acronyms). Diana was not done. She had an insatiable desire to swim all the way from Cuba to Key West, Florida. Ms. Nyad wanted to be the first person to make this seemingly impossible 110-mile swim, without using the aid of a protective shark cage. Talk about a lofty goal!

She first tried in 1978 and she was able to complete 68 miles before strong winds forced her to stop. Over 30 years would pass before Diana gave it another shot. By this time Diana was in her 60s. Can you imagine how much life took place during those 3 decades? No matter how many different things she accomplished between that time, there was still a void within her because the job was not complete.

I started to see myself in Diana. Yes, I won a new car from rapping; an accomplishment so unique that I'm unaware of any other person in existence that has done it. Yes, I won an all-expense paid trip to New York, not once but two years in a row, from spitting a one-minute verse. Those two stories are already feathers in my cap that one day I'll be able to tell my granddaughter. Athens, as she sits in my lap in my favorite rocking chair. Nyad could have settled in the same way when she swam around Manhattan and from the Bahamas to Florida. However, she knew there was more to accomplish. There was more work to be done. New levels to reach. New York and a new car were not enough for me, either.

The second year that I went to the Big Apple, they brought Fat Joe in as a mentor for the finalists. His job was to offer advice and to provide both positive and constructive feedback on our performances. We had the pleasure of participating in a freestyle cipher with the Bronx native at the end of taping. I rhymed immediately after Fat Joe spit his verse. Later that evening one of the VH-1 producers gave me a call. He told me that he was on the elevator with Fat Joe as they were leaving the building and the Terror Squad emcee said to him "Yo, everyone was nice, but that big dude? WHOA! He was a problem!"

The joy I felt when I heard that is hard to even put into words. To have a hip-hop legend like Fat Joe, who was born in the birthplace of hip-hop, notice and acknowledge my skills was an enormous confidence boost. I could have packed up my bags at that point and came back home to St. Pete with infinite bragging rights, yet I wasn't satisfied. The goal of being a full-time songwriter and artist had yet to materialize.

Diana faced all kinds of obstacles when she re-attempted that swim. She failed time after time, due to storms, deadly jellyfish stings and more. So many people, including her best friend, tried to get her to quit. They meant well. They didn't want her to lose her very life, trying to prove something that didn't need to be proved. Diana Nyad was stubborn. She refused to let sharks, jellyfish, bad weather or anything else get in the way of fulfilling her dream. How often do we allow the sharks of this world to stop us from getting to the other side? We don't know how close we are to that breakthrough and we never will if we continue to put it into reverse instead of leaving it in drive.

After 5 failed attempts, Diana Nyad completed the impossible at age 64 – she finished a 110 mile long, 52-hour swim from Cuba to Florida, in the open sea, with no protective shark cage! There were fans, friends, family and reporters, all cheering her on when she walked ashore, fatigued, famished, but finally victorious. I was so inspired as I sat in awe, watching my television screen. This was the second time in my life that I was moved to write a song after watching a revelatory film.

The first movie to affect me in such a way was *Star Wars: Revenge of The Sith.* Shortly after coming in 2nd place in the VH-1 competition, I found myself on the couch, watching my feelings and emotions play out right before my eyes on a Star Wars DVD. Anakin Skywalker began as one of the good guys. He wanted to do what was right, but he was constantly being tempted by the dark side. By the end of the movie, it was abundantly clear that this was my experience and how I felt when I didn't come in first place in that competition. I remember thinking to myself "Maybe I should have used foul language like the guy who won the contest did." After all, the grand prize was $10,000, plus a sit down with a label executive. The money would have been great but the chance to show a big-time industry executive what I could do was right there at my fingertips and I let it slip away, all because I chose not to cuss. I saw myself in Anakin, so I quickly picked up a pen and began to write. Sometimes it seems like the bad guys always win, while the good guys get shafted. The disappointment and discouragement were so palpable that I ended up writing a song called "Anakin" to get my feelings out into the atmosphere. In the first verse I take on the role of the tempting Sith Lord, trying to lure Anakin over to the dark side. The second verse finds me rapping as Anakin himself, resisting the enticement of going from good to bad. To this day it is my son's favorite song by me, and it is available both at www.shadcore.com and on my "Shadcore" SoundCloud page, if you would like to download it.

Now, 18 years later, Diana Nyad's story has touched me in a similar way. Nyad is Shadcore and Shadcore is Nyad. It feels like I've been swimming through shark-infested waters for years, desperately trying to reach the shore of songwriting success. I am grateful for both of my jobs, as they keep a roof over my family's head and food on our table, but I know that I was created with a greater purpose. My desire is to earn an abundant living, solely from my gift as a writer. I've seen on too many occasions how my words and my voice inspired others. I was made for this. It's my destiny to, figuratively, swim from Cuba to Florida.

The *Nyad* movie had to be told in rhyme form and it had to be told by me. I needed the right production, so I began sifting through emails from one of the "cold email producers." Ask any artist and they'll tell you when you know, you know. I went through a few different options before coming across the winning track. The bassline was bouncy, and I loved how the drums swung. The music sounded introspective enough for an artist to bare their soul on. I quickly shot the Ukrainian producer, Svgar, an email to make sure the track had not been purchased yet. Once he assured me the track was still available, I sent him the money, via PayPal, for the instrumental and I threw on my thinking cap.

Usually (for me at least), the opening line is the most difficult to create. You want to grab the listener's attention; therefore, some significant thought has to go into those first few words. Once I came up with *"Too blessed to be stressed, swam from Cuba to Key West,"* I knew I was on to something special. Every line afterwards just seemed to flow, like Nyad in the open sea. I experimented with a slightly behind the beat type of flow that I hadn't tried before and to my surprise it worked like a charm!

In the same way the film inspired me to write a song, I wanted to pay that forward and inspire the listener to stay in pursuit of their passion and purpose. Although this song can provide motivation at any age level, I had my age and peer group specifically in mind when I wrote it. We put certain timelines in our heads of when a dream or goal should be achieved and when we don't hit those deadlines, we tend to get frustrated and give up.

Hip-Hop has always been deemed a young man's game. I remember being 21 years old and thinking, "I sure hope I'm signed by the time I reach 25." Then 25 came and the new goal was to be on by 30. Here I am knocking on 50's door and I'm still trying to score that touchdown. When I look at Hip-Hop music today, though, I can't help but notice the emcees making some of the best music are all well into their 50s! Folks like Nas, Common, Black Thought, Busta Rhymes, Goodie Mob, Snoop Dogg, Eminem and my favorite, Rakim, all have crossed the half century mark, yet this is some of the best music they've made in their careers. If they can still do it, why can't I? Besides, I've never lost the passion so, if the fire continues to burn inside, I have no intentions of quelching it.

When I completed the two verses, along with the hook, it still felt like there was a component missing. One day it just hit me out of the blue – I need to have Diana's voice on the song! I began searching YouTube to see if, maybe, she gave a speech or two regarding her story. Lo and behold, I found a TED TALK that she did, and I listened from start to finish to see if she said anything that would put a bow on this well-crafted composition. To my enjoyment there were several nuggets for me to choose from, so I decided to start and end the song with snippets from that speech. It turned out perfect and the confirmation for me was when my daughter, Tasanee, asked if I could email her an early copy of the song because she loved it that much. She even pointed out the behind-the-beat flow! I hope Diana Nyad, herself, hears this song one day, just so she knows how much she inspired me. She made me want to swim some extra laps, for sure.

CHAPTER 4:
Stress Relief
(Acupressure)

I have to level with you. It's not easy working two jobs, being a husband and a father, all while trying to stay motivated to pursue your passion. I've had plenty of co-workers ask, "How do you have time to write songs and make music?" Admittedly, I don't even know the answer to that question. The thing that I'm most passionate about doesn't quite pay the bills right now, so I must do what I must do. In a perfect world I'd spend those 12 hours I work every day in the studio instead. I would be on stage for at least 3 nights a week. Prayerfully, that day will come, but until it does, this present grind is my reality. I try not to do it begrudgingly because I know there are less fortunate people out there who would love to just have a job, let alone two. However, trying to juggle this type of workload can bring on a tremendous amount of stress. It's extremely important to be cognizant of that fact so that you know how to properly manage it.

Stress can literally take you off this earth if you allow it to. It has negative effects on our bodies, leading to things like ulcers and hypertension. Indulging in addictive behaviors is often a direct result of stress in our lives. It can also lead to insomnia and so many other issues that are not beneficial to healthy living. For us to overcome stress we must combat it head on.

Stress relief can come in several different forms, and you may have to experiment a little to find out what works best for you. For some it may be going for a brisk walk or jog, while it might mean paying a visit to the gun range for others. Maybe a short vacation will do the trick. Hopefully reading this book could serve as a stress reliever. The important thing is to recognize when you are becoming stressed or overwhelmed and to respond accordingly.

I was recently asked to bring the message at my church for Father's Day. Shortly after being requested to speak, I had a dream and when I awoke, I knew exactly what God wanted the message to be about –Peace. He pointed me to John 14:27 –"Peace I leave with you, my peace I give unto you: Let not your heart be troubled, neither let it be afraid." This was the foundational scripture that I taught from. Jesus was preparing His disciples for His departure but letting them know that He was sending the Holy Spirit to comfort them in His physical absence. He didn't want them to be troubled nor overtaken with stress.

As I was studying in preparation for the sermon, it was alarming, to say the least, to discover how many people in this country suffer from anxiety. The "1 in every 5 persons" ratio was staggering. The good thing about stress, though, is you don't have to stay there. It's not a permanent destination. Just as Jesus was reassuring His disciples that He had a solution for their worries, the same is true for you and me today.

Prayer is one of the best stress relievers that I know of. Having a great relationship with God will put things in perspective for you. What we war with goes far beyond what we can see in the natural realm. Even with this knowledge, however, I'm still human, so stress tries to attack me just the same. I am in no way exempt. Most who know me will say I'm a pretty optimistic guy, but I do get stressed at times.

I wanted to express that reality when I wrote "Acupressure". I knew that I wanted to feature my good friend and bandmate, Eliana B., on the chorus for this record. Her voice was sent straight from heaven! She has unbelievable range and control over the tone of her voice. My goal was to paint the picture of a hard-working man coming home from a grueling shift. When he arrives, he enters a tranquil, much more forgiving, setting, where his woman greets him with love, affection and a much-needed neck massage.

This realistic contrast of mayhem and peace is what I felt when I first heard the beat. This track was produced by Svgar, the same producer from the Ukraine who produced "NYAD." I liked his work so much that he ended up producing nearly half of the album! One of his signature instruments is the Spanish guitar. His use of it on this song reminded me of something you might hear upon entering a massage parlor. It was relaxing and serene, while the drums were busy in a hustle and bustle, rat race kind of way. I believe that duality is what planted the seed, subconsciously, to write on this specific topic.

Like I mentioned before, I knew Eliana needed to be on this song with me. Her voice is calm and soothing just like a good massage. We've collaborated since 2011 when we met in a music program at Saint Petersburg College. There is no genre of music that she can't master. I've heard her sing R&B, Jazz, Pop, Rock, Funk, you name it! For me, as a songwriter, she is a complete joy to work with. I've been able to explore the depths of my writing because she's willing to deliver a stellar performance, no matter what style I present her with.

This song was written, specifically, with the fellas in mind. I wanted to give a voice to the type of guy who sacrifices, works hard for his family and all he wants in return is a little appreciation. There's nothing quite like coming home to some peace and tranquility after spending all day in utter chaos. The stress relief in this scenario is the soft hands of his woman providing an acupressure neck massage. As men, sometimes physical touch is all that's required to ease the stress. We want to be seen, heard and cared for as well. That massage is doing just as much for us mentally and emotionally as it is physically. Actions speak way louder than words. While we do enjoy hearing "baby, I appreciate you," it hits a lot different when you have a bath drawn, candles lit, a hot meal and a soothing rub down awaiting you when you walk through the door!

I complimented Eliana on her incredible performance right after she laid it down and it prompted an interesting discussion. I told her how convincing she sounded singing what I wrote, and she attributed it to her experience as a young child who did a ton of musical theater. She believes that helped her learn how to connect with the characters in order to effectively convey what they were trying to say. Beforehand, she asked exactly how I wanted her to sing her part. By using the softer tone, it showed a level of sensitivity to her man's plight. The words on the chorus are *"I know the price you pay, working all night and day. Your plate's in the microwave and I can warm it up for you. I'm here to ease your stress. Let me massage your neck. You deserve nothing less. I appreciate what you do."* Now imagine hearing those same words, but in a soft, calming voice, when you enter the front door. It doesn't matter how bad your day was going up to that point because it would instantly improve if you were greeted in this way.

Eliana and I have chemistry because we have so much history of collaborating. We both want what's best for the record so that allows us to bounce ideas off one another. It was her idea to add *"This is how I say 'thank you'"* to the second and final hook, as opposed to *"I appreciate what you do,"* which is what I initially wrote and what we used on the first chorus. She felt it helped to push the story along. I completely agreed. I love when she's invested in the music because she can see things that I might miss. It's crucial, not only as an artist but as a person in general, to remain coachable and be willing to learn. Someone may have an idea that can take your idea to the next level. If you insist on everything being your way, then you will miss out. This is what makes my friend and I such a great team. We trust each other, creatively, and we each know what the other brings to the table.

A fun fact about "Acupressure" is this was not the original title of the song. I originally titled it "Neck Massage" but after we recorded it, I felt like that title was a little too "on the nose." So, I decided to google different types of massages to try to draw inspiration for a new title. When I came across the word "acupressure," " it sounded a lot more enticing. It's weird, but just by changing the title made the song sound better to me. The word "acupressure" provided the curiosity I like to create when I come up with my titles.

Another fun fact is this was not the original song I had in mind for Eliana and me to record for the album. Originally, I wrote a song called "Crave." It was also produced by Svgar and it had an Afro Beats or Caribbean vibe to it. "Crave" was written by me, but mostly featured Eliana B., while I provided a rap for the second verse. My long-time friend O.G., who you'll learn more about in Chapter 7, texted me one day and suggested I let Eliana use it as her song, featuring me, instead of the other way around. He said it sounded more like it should be her song since she was featured more.

At first, I disagreed. I realized she was the lead actor, while I played more of a supportive role, but that was by design. I wanted to showcase my talent as a writer who could write outside of the hip-hop genre with the "Crave" record. I thought about what O.G. said over the next few days and I eventually concluded that he was right.

I had other plans for "Crave." I remembered that I had previously written and recorded an R&B song called "Do What You Do" that featured my partner, Theo Lane, and Eliana on it. I'm not featured on this song at all. I started thinking since I have this song and "Crave" already recorded, I can write one or two more songs and put them all on an EP that highlights my songwriter side.

But I still needed a mid-to-up-tempo song, with my sis on the album. I patiently waited for an email to come from Svgar, who usually sends 10 beats at a time. About two weeks after I pulled "Crave" from the track list, I got the email I was waiting for. I sifted through each individual beat until I heard the "Acupressure" beat. I knew Eliana's voice would sound incredible over this music. All I had to do was make sure to switch our roles to indicate that I was the lead, while she was the support this time and we were good to go.

My wife would, again, serve as my muse for this song. She is a great stress reliever. Sometimes all it takes is a simple smile or a certain look that communicates to me, "I see you" or "I'm here for you." Having this wonderful woman in my life, who understands my plight, is such a blessing. It's very easy to write these types of songs because I draw from real life experience. My wife knows there is no shame in catering to your man. Whether it's a hug, shoulder rub or washing my back in the tub, she's down to help reduce the stress in my life. She also provides me with spiritual acupressure, just like the Comforter did for the disciples, and for that I say Amen!

CHAPTER 5:
Partner in Rhyme
(Sam & Denzel)

When two iron blades rub together their blades become sharper, in essence making them more effective, hence the biblical phrase "iron sharpens iron." This truth is the reason I frequently collaborate with my homie and partner-in-rhyme, Jay Acolyte AKA J. Ack. We met back in 2011 as attendants of St. Petersburg College. We were enrolled in their music program, Music Industry Recording Arts (MIRA). It didn't take long for us to discover that we were both emcees, who shared an equal passion for writing and rhyming.

In early 2012, Jay had an epiphany that helped usher in a new sound to the Tampa Bay area, which has left an indelible mark in my hometown that is still felt to this day. Up until that time the MIRA program had a handful of music ensembles that encouraged students to collaborate with one another in different music genres. So, there were Rock, Jazz, Pop and R&B ensembles already in operation. In these ensembles the students typically spent the semester learning how to play cover songs in their respective genres. One day Jay approached me and said he wanted to ask the professors about including a hip-hop ensemble into the curriculum. He wanted to know if I would like to be a part of it. Honestly, I thought the idea was genius. The idea was for us to assemble some of our classmates in an attempt to create some original compositions throughout the semester and then perform them live at the end of the term in front of faculty and staff. Each student would receive an elective credit based on how well we executed the assignment.

Prior to this program, for the most part, I wrote my rhymes to an existing instrumental track that was created with virtual instruments. Being in this program was my introduction to writing songs with actual musicians. During middle school, I played percussion in the symphonic band. But we weren't writing our own material back then. We played whatever was on the sheet music in front of us. This was a new experience for me, and I loved it! Hip-Hop music is primarily loop based, meaning the same music pattern usually repeats every four to eight measures. Now I was working with real musicians and there was a freedom to experiment with chord progressions, time signatures and key changes that regular rap beats didn't provide. What we could not predict when we first assembled was the level of chemistry we developed almost instantly. Jay and I handled writing the lyrics, while the musicians took care of composing the music. We needed a name to call ourselves, so I came up with 'Clash of The Titans' since the school mascot was "Titans." One student suggested "The Real Clash of The Titans" because we are actual people and not mythical gods. We went with that name for a few months before we shortened it to just "The Real Clash." When it was time to perform at the end of the semester to determine our grade, we had already written 7 songs! We put on an amazing show, so much so that the professors approached us at the end and told us we'd be doing ourselves and the community a disservice if we didn't continue as a band. They told us to take our talents outside the four walls of the campus so that we could truly make a name for ourselves. We took their advice and began to wreak havoc all over Tampa Bay for the next several years.

In 2014 we were named "Best of The Bay" for hip-hop ensemble by Creative Loafing of Tampa, as well as being featured on the cover of their publication for the December 05, 2013 issue. Our biggest accomplishment came in 2017 when we competed in a national competition for the opportunity to earn a spot to play at the Okeechobee Music Festival. We came in first place and ended up performing on the same bill with Usher, The Roots, Wiz Khalifa, Logic, George Clinton, Anderson .Paak and Kings of Leon! Over the years we have had some musician changes, but all of the vocalists are original members – Jay, Eliana B. and me.

Through it all, Jay and I have continued to work with one another. This is my fourth solo album since we met and Jay is featured on each one of them. I make sure to include him on my projects because I know he is going to "push my pen." I know we tend to bring the best out of each other because we are both highly skilled when it comes to putting words and ideas together. I want to work with someone who challenges me to take my artistry to the next level and Jay does that. Everyone can use a partner in rhyme. It doesn't have to be in music. For you it may be a gym buddy. It might be a study partner for someone else. The point is that you have that special person in your life that inspires you to be your best self. We've become more than just rhyme partners over these past 13 years. Jay is my brother from another. Our wives have become great friends as well. We can talk about anything without judgment and we know when we collaborate, we can expect greatness to come from both sides.

When it came time to feature Jay on the album, I wanted to go outside of what we normally did together. In the past, be it for The Real Clash or for my solo projects, we usually would resort to positive themes or creative fun stories for the subject matter. To that point I recently had a conversation with my friend, JC, who was introduced to my music around the beginnings of The Real Clash. He made a comment, upon hearing some of the music from *I Left a Mess in There,* that I sounded more like I would take your head off now than I did some years back. He was curious to know what had changed. I had to think about it for a minute. I told him that this album was more of a return to my roots as a dangerous emcee; one not to be taken lightly. JC had never heard that side of me because I tucked that guy away when I started with The Real Clash. Our music was focused more on positivity, fun and good vibes so with that I suppressed my Hulk-like persona for the greater good of the group. My brother wasn't familiar with the 'Brutal' version of Shadcore. I knew that Jay possessed an inner-Hulk in him as well and I wanted us both to release the "green guy" on this song.

Even though this track was all about showcasing bars it still had to be different. It had to be special because, after all, it's featuring the same genius who introduced a hip-hop curriculum to a collegiate program! I'm always brainstorming and trying to come up with new concepts to write about so I began thinking about dynamic duos who Jay and I might have something in common with. I thought about Shaq and Kobe, but I quickly threw that idea into the recycle bin because J. Ack isn't a huge sports guy. "Well, what do Jay and I have in common?" I pondered. We both like movies. This thought immediately made me think about my favorite two actors– Denzel Washington and Samuel L. Jackson. Now I started feeling like I was heading in the right direction. I love unique and original song titles. In fact, a pet peeve of mine is when I hear unimaginative, lazy, overused song title choices. This is J. Ack and Shadcore! This is Sam and Denzel! BOOM! There we go. Now we're cooking with grease! Two of the best at their craft. These two actors have earned the right for fans to come in droves to the theaters to view their performances, simply because they're featured in them.

When you hear the names Samuel L. Jackson and Denzel Washington, you're instantly intrigued. Those brothers have so much depth between them, and they are so far ahead of their counterparts that I consider them to be peerless. Well, that describes J. Ack and me in a nutshell. "How do we drive this point home and hit the nail on the head?" I thought to myself. I came up with a dope idea shortly after that thought. We are going to reference their movie titles, respectfully in our verses, to let people know we are not to be messed with! So, I will take on the role of Denzel and Jay will do the same for Samuel.

I really get excited to write once I have developed a concrete concept. It's one thing to use references to complete a verse, but when you can creatively tell a story, using nothing but the movie titles from an actor's catalog, that's a different level of artistry. I wrote my verse in under 30 minutes then I sent it to Jay, along with the beat and a voice memo explaining the concept. He hit me back and told me he loved the beat and the idea and that the beat was different from what I normally rapped over. Jay also pointed out the "Reading Rainbow" sample that was used in the track. I hadn't even noticed but I took it as confirmation that we were about to educate folks on the art of lyricism.

The first line of the hook summarizes the entire song. "Pros don't hang where the amateurs dwell." As they often say, there are levels to this. This was the whole point I wanted to establish from the get-go. We are not your average rappers, just as Sam and Denzel are not your average actors. The final ingredient for this dish was the voices of both thespians. I wanted to make sure we grabbed a couple of iconic one-liners, so I went with "Yes, they deserve to die and I hope they burn in hell!' from 'A Time To Kill' to start Jay's verse and "I wish you had more time" from 'Man on Fire' to end my verse.

Of all of our collaborations, "Sam & Denzel" is my favorite because we are both in our element, slaying whatever and whoever gets in our path. We left a mess in there on this one. Two partners in rhyme, helping to sharpen the other's iron. Don't get too close or you might get cut!

by RASHAD "SHADCORE" HARRELL

CHAPTER 6:
Thanks, Dad!
(The Florida Room)

I'll never forget February 25, 2014. I was on the computer at the public library, and I had just sent my dad a message, asking him if he saw me on TV the day before. Our band, The Real Clash, performed live on a local channel and I was hoping my hero had the chance to see his son do what he loved doing the most. I didn't wait for a response because I knew I had a long walk to get back home. My car wasn't working at the time and if you know anything about this Florida heat, then even in the winter you know it's no joke! I wasn't home for a good thirty minutes when I received a call that no child ever wants to receive. My mother was on the other line, crying frantically, saying that my dad was unresponsive and that I needed to get to the hospital immediately. I'm getting teary-eyed as I recall this memory. My dad had just suffered a massive heart attack. When I arrived at the hospital and saw my mother, Auntie Darlene, and Uncle Bruce all crying, I knew it wasn't good, but when my aunt said, "He's gone!" I collapsed to my knees and began wailing. Seeing the pain on my mother's face and knowing there was nothing I could do to console her was a sting that I have never felt before. This was, by far, the toughest thing I had ever endured. My dad was my real-life superhero. He was a great father and a loving husband. I aspired to grow up to be like him in many ways.

It's been 10 years since his passing and I'm in a much better place, spiritually and emotionally. I used to ask myself, "Shad, when are you gonna pay tribute to your dad in a song?" I've done many tributes in the past for other friends and family members. When my Auntie Val was tragically murdered in 1995, I wrote and recorded a song in her honor. I made a song for my friend and fellow church member, Johnny, when he passed in 2004. I couldn't put my finger on it as to why I hadn't honored my dad in this way until I wrote "The Florida Room." I believe, subconsciously, I knew that penning a song in remembrance of my father meant it was real and a painful reminder that he truly was no longer with us. I wanted to keep him alive in my heart.

While there will never be a time that I'm completely over it, I will say that I have done a great job coping with my father's absence. I thank God for the 38 years that I got to spend with my hero. I'm appreciative of his presence in my life and in our household because that was not the reality for a lot of my friends and family, unfortunately. I also never wanted to "force" writing a tribute just for the sake of writing one. If it was going to happen, it had to happen organically. Well guess what? Pops was an organic farmer, so it made sense on the natural process of how this composition came to be.

Before I wrote this song, I thought my album was complete. I had written the other 14 songs and had beats already pre-selected for all of them. Studio time was booked ahead of time for the final 3 songs I had to record. On a warm July afternoon, my go-to producer, Troy Cedeño of the C-Lab Productions, messaged me to let me know there was a new composition sitting in my email for me to check out.

Before I go any further, let me tell you about my friend, Troy. We met back in 2017. At the time there was a local artist by the name of Ari Chi, who had just released her debut album, *Color Fool.* I was familiar with her because my band, The Real Clash, had shared a bill with her before. She's an amazing singer and ukulele player. I had been anticipating her album drop and since the only instrument I ever heard accompanying her was the ukulele, that's exactly what I was looking forward to hearing on her album. Her voice and a single instrument were all she needed to make a memorable project. Much to my surprise the songs were all fully fleshed out, complete with drums, bass, guitar, piano, horns and more! So, like I used to do with my daddy's vinyl records, I looked up the album's digital liner notes. I saw that the album was produced by a guy named Troy Cedeño. I had to reach out and let this dude know how well the album was produced and mixed. I also wanted him to know that he had just gained a new fan for life.

Even though her album sounded like a fresh take on Neo-Soul, I could tell that Troy knew a thing or two about Hip-Hop, based on the drums alone. We sparked up a conversation, via messenger, and the next thing you know I was at his studio, working out ideas for some new Shadcore music.

For me, Troy is the best of both worlds- he's a musician who knows how to produce! I've worked with others in the past who were good at one, but not necessarily the other. With Troy, I have the luxury of recording non-loop-based material, as a solo artist, without the cumbersome workload that comes with recording an entire band. It's a lot easier to get stuff done when working with one individual, as opposed to getting the schedules of a seven-piece band to align.

Originally, we were planning on doing a 3 to 5 song EP, but when you get a couple of creatives in a room together, dope things tend to happen and sometimes it's difficult to put a cap on it. Before I knew it, I had recorded a full-length album, produced solely by Troy Cedeño! That album is available for streaming today. It's called *Frisson*, by yours truly, Shadcore.

Now let's get back to the story. When I opened the email to hear the new track Troy sent, it instantly took me somewhere. I couldn't quite put a finger on it, but I knew that I was transported to a different time and place when I listened to this music. The more I played the instrumental the more that time and place revealed itself and, by the end of the day, I knew exactly where it had taken me to— The Florida Room! If you could only hear the enthusiasm in my voice when I sent him a voice memo saying, "Troy, I'm gonna call this song 'The Florida Room' and I'm gonna talk about all that good music my dad used to play in there!"

We listened to music all the time, as a family, growing up. The Florida Room was surrounded with records, reel-to-reel machines, stereo receivers, tape cases full of cassettes and huge floor model speakers. Art was plastered on the walls as well as family photo collages. My dad was in the service and was stationed in Germany, which meant he had access to some of the world's best stereo equipment. As many of his close friends will tell you, Pops changed the game when he brought that equipment back home. No one around had the gear my dad possessed, including the music. He had all kinds of imports and limited releases that only a few could get their hands on.

There was always some kind of music playing in the house. Parties, family gatherings, no matter the occasion, music stayed in rotation. Pops played everything, too. The Rolling Stones, Funkadelic, The Jackson 5, Phil Collins, Stevie Wonder, you name it, we heard it in the Florida Room.

I wanted to recapture that feeling on this song. I wanted to grab the listener by the hand, hop in my time travel machine, and invite them to a time when that room was booming with good music! They were welcome to get on the dancefloor and "cut a rug" or they could have a seat in my dad's favorite recliner to just sit and soak up the sounds. Take in the moment. Enjoy the experience and become inspired like I did. I was a sponge, absorbing all the different grooves and melodies that were entering my ear gates. I felt the bass as it reverberated in my chest. I was fascinated by the stories and the way the words rhymed together. Whether he knew it or not, my dad was helping me to discover my passion. Some of my fondest memories occurred in that room.

I realized once I had the concept for the record that this was going to be the way I finally honored my father in song. He was such an interesting man that I could have, literally, talked about a hundred different ways he impacted my life, but this is what I felt compelled to write about. This song went right along with the theme of the album – to leave a mess in there! To make a difference. To shift the atmosphere. My dad left a beautiful mess. I thanked Troy for sending this track because the album wouldn't have been complete without it.

Not only would the album be incomplete, but it would have had a totally different album cover. It wasn't until I wrote "The Florida Room" that I thought about looking through my mom's old photo albums for potential pics to use as artwork for the single. I thought if I decided to use this song as the single, it would be dope to have a pic of my father, standing in the Florida Room next to his stereo. When I mentioned the idea to my mother, she knew exactly where to find such a picture!

I took a picture of the picture and sent it to a few of my homeboys. I told them that this was the pic I was thinking about using for artwork for "The Florida Room." The more I stared at the photo the more it became apparent to me that this was, indeed, the actual cover for the album! I look so much like my father, so looking at this young picture of him made me feel like I was looking at myself. Also, the way he's looking back at the camera sort of suggests that he's saying to the camera *"I left a mess in there"* when I made Rashad. He's a game-changer. He's special and he's going to impact the world one day. I left a legacy that I am proud of.

When I heard the music, I knew just the artist I wanted to feature on it. It sounded like something Marvin Gaye would sing over, so I had to call up the most soulful singer I know –- my brother, Theo Lane. Theo grew up on great music, as well. He and I met in 2016 at a music awards event in Tampa. We both knew of each other, just from being a part of the local music scene, so it was a pleasure to finally meet in person. We had talked about the possibility of a collaboration, but nothing materialized for the first two years. It wasn't until our songs were played, back-to-back, on the radio that I reached back out and said let's really make something happen this time.

I called him up when my friend and former Tampa Bay Buccaneer, Ian Beckles, was looking to make a song that showcased the variety of musical talent in the Tampa Bay area. Ian wanted me to handpick the artists that were going to be featured on the song because he knew that this was my area of expertise. This was the perfect opportunity to finally link up with Theo, and he came in and shut it all the way down, with a fire verse and powerful ad libs for the chorus, alongside Eliana B. I called him again for a song off my *Frisson* album called, "Pheromones." My daughter, Kailey, loves that song.

Theo is not only a dope singer, but he is also an incredible songwriter, as well. What I love about working with him is his positive energy and his lack of ego. Even though he writes on his own, he's always down to let me write for him and because we've worked together so often, I know how to write, specifically for his voice.

I wanted Theo to channel his inner Marvin Gaye for "The Florida Room." I needed it to feel like Marvin returned, just to be featured on this dedication song with me. Theo did what he usually does and took the song into a different stratosphere, with his tone, signature runs and soulful harmonies.

It may have taken 10 years to immortalize my Pops on record, but this is precisely how and when it was supposed to happen. I'm at peace with that. My dad was a remarkable man, so a song in his honor could not be anything short of remarkable.

CHAPTER 7:
Adjust
(Merge Left)

I was on my way to Wal-Mart, one day, and I saw a sign that read "merge left." Now, I take the same route every time I go to this Wal-Mart but, on this day, the sign stuck out to me and it sparked an idea for a new song. It was as if God was showing me a metaphor for life. In a perfect world we would live our lives with zero resistance, all gas and no breaks, but the truth is we constantly must adjust. Be adaptable if you want to thrive. If we don't "merge left" then we'll eventually run out of road and the traffic of life will pass us by.

The ideas started coming as fast as the cars on the highway that day. I began to reflect on myself, as it pertained to me remaining relevant as a rapper approaching his 50s. I've had to adjust to the evolution of hip-hop music, whether willingly or reluctantly. Change is inevitable. We often dislike the idea of change because it disrupts our norm. As time passes, we tend to snuggle into our comfort zones. When the opportunity of change presents itself, the initial response is usually one of resistance. The unknown can be a scary place, but what's even scarier is allowing fear to dictate how we move, or don't move.

So, what do I mean by "my relevance as a rapper nearing his 50s"? As I alluded to before, rap has always been deemed a young man's sport so by that standard alone, my window should have closed a couple of decades ago. My friend, Bongo, recently asked me, "Bro, how is your writing *still* improving after all these years?" I told him it's because I still enjoy the craft of songwriting. Even though I've worked on my art for quite some time, I know that there is still room for improvement. There are still adjustments I can make to get better.

My favorite line from my verse on "Merge Left" is "And I still ain't even wrote my dopest verse yet!" This line summarizes my mentality as a writer. I always believe that I can outdo the last line I wrote. What that looks like in the natural realm is finding new ways to create. Is there a pocket I can flow in that I have yet to attempt? What are some words I can utilize that I've never used before? What new subject matters should I tackle? What stories haven't been told yet?

I've always felt the rappers who have stood the test of time and remained the most relevant were the ones who knew how to merge left. Look at Nas for example. He has had a few resurgences throughout his lengthy career. Perhaps his most notable move was his recent collaboration with his much younger, West Coast affiliated producer, Hit-Boy. To some, this may have seemed like an unlikely pairing. An O.G. legend from New York, working with a young producer from California? How is *that* supposed to sound? Nevertheless, Nas followed his gut and he merged left. It proved to be the right decision because this partnership earned Nas his first Grammy for Best Rap Album in 2021, twenty-seven years after his debut was released!

Busta Rhymes is another artist who comes to mind when I think of longevity and relevance. To this day, he is one of the most sought-after emcees, when it comes to guest features. In fact, in my humble opinion, Busta is the king of the "feature verse." His two most iconic features are 20 years apart – 1991's "The Scenario" by *A Tribe Called Quest* and 2011's "Look At Me Now" by *Chris Brown*. Busta Rhymes was never the "get off my lawn" type of elder emcee. He has always embraced and worked with the younger generation. His original group was called *Leaders of The New School* and Busta is living up to that name as he continues to lead by example. There are a host of others that have consistently reinvented themselves like LL Cool J, Common, Snoop Dogg and Black Thought, just to name a few.

My brother, good friend and fellow group member, O.G. The Originaal, immediately came to mind when I thought about who I would like to feature on this song. There are only a few remaining in my peer group, who actively create and pursue music on a consistent basis. O.G. is one of the last standing from a certain era.

We met over 20 years ago, while working at a call center together. I was selling magazine subscriptions and O.G. worked in the mailroom. We bonded instantly due to our mutual love for rapping. During our breaks we would both participate in freestyle rap ciphers and we agreed to get into the studio together to work on some music. Our intentions were great, but we ended up losing contact after I got a new job, so it seemed as if the collaboration was not going to happen. However, God's timing is always perfect because, nearly 20 years later, O.G. and I reconnected and we weren't going to let this opportunity pass us by. We had to merge left this time.

We talked about some ideas and we, finally, got our first song recorded together when he featured me on his solo album, *Never Quit*. The chemistry and mutual respect were so evident that we decided to form a group together, but we needed one more piece to complete the assignment. I suggested we reach out to my homie, Theo Lane, to see if he was down to join us. I knew O.G. was already a fan of Theo's music from hearing the collaboration Theo and I did for my song "Pheromones." I felt like Theo's smooth R&B voice was a perfect complement and balance for our aggressive flows.

Before forming the group, O.G. and I were going to write a song called, "Kings Recognize Kings" so, when it was time to come up with a group name, I said let's go with that, or KRK for short. Theo and O.G. both loved the idea, and it was one of the best decisions I've ever made, because the brotherhood we've formed since uniting is an unbreakable one. We talk all the time, bouncing ideas off one another. We truly have each other's interests at heart, not just as artists, but as men, period. We're all happily married, family men, who religiously recognize each other as kings.

I knew O.G. was perfect for this song, because he writes as much as I do and he's in his mid-50s! What I love about my brother is his honesty and humility. With O.G., what you see is what you get. He is in constant pursuit of being a better person and a better artist. In order to achieve that goal means having a willingness to adjust. Remember, merge left, or let life pass you by.

Once I knew O.G. would be my guest, it was then just a matter of picking out the right track for the song. What gravitated me toward the instrumental I chose was its striking resemblance to something 2Pac would rap over. The piano melody was fused with Pac-like energy and, knowing that Mr. Shakur is O.G. 's favorite rapper, I felt strongly like he would like the track as much as I did. He hit me back, confirming my suspicion, and he wrote his verse the same day.

Some months would pass before we laid the song down and that's a funny story, by itself. One day, J. Ack, O.G. and I, were in the studio, working on our side project, *THREE!* "Three" is an acronym for These Hungry Rappers Eat Everything. We finished recording our song, "Alter-Ego" a lot sooner than we anticipated, so we had some extra time to work on additional material. I asked O.G. if he wanted to knock out "Merge Left" before we left. Now, remember earlier I said that O.G. writes as much as I do, but our processes are a lot different. I usually record a voice memo on my phone after writing the words down on paper. By doing so, I can listen to the demo over and over, while driving in the car or on my headphones, and this helps me memorize the words. Once the verse is committed to memory, the paper becomes obsolete, so it's likely I may toss it. No big deal. O.G., on the other hand is extremely organized (probably due to his military background), and since he writes so often, he doesn't normally memorize his verses because he can always refer to his notebook when it's time to record or recite them. When I asked him if he wanted to record "Merge Left," he said, "Man, you should have told me before I left the crib!" Well, the "crib" was all the way back in Orlando, and the studio we were recording in was in Clearwater, Florida! For those of you who don't know, that's not exactly right around the corner, so he couldn't just go and grab it quickly. However, O.G. merged left and made a quick adjustment. He texted his wife and since he knew the notebook's exact location, due to his organizational skills, he directed her to the verse and asked her to take a picture and forward it to him. Thanks to him being fast on his feet, I didn't have to schedule a new session to record the song and we knocked it out the same day. We killed two birds with one stone and saved me some money in the process.

Speaking of Pac, I was trying to channel his energy in my verse. I wanted the listener to hear the urgency in my voice and to realize the importance of adjusting to improve yourself. Even as I'm writing this book, adjustments are being made along the way. Sure, you're either reading or listening to the finished product, but if you saw the rough draft, I doubt that you'd be able to interpret it. There are so many lines that have been scratched through, written over, added and omitted, that it's ridiculous.

That's what I love about it, though. I welcome all the mistakes. This pruning must occur, so that you receive it in its shiniest, most presentable form. We don't always get it right on our first attempt and, even if we do, things are subject to change. Such is life. As we age, we aren't going to do the same things, physically, that we used to do.

The great Michael Jordan comes to mind when I think of this. Early in his career, MJ was flying through the air, dunking on any and everyone who got in his way. His sheer athleticism was enough to dominate most of his opponents. Father Time eventually caught up with him, as those dunks became fewer and fewer by the game. MJ decided to merge left. He developed a new way to dominate in the form of the "fadeaway jumper." This move was just as unstoppable as those electrifying dunks but catered more for an aging athlete.

What adjustments are you making today to remain effective? Only you can answer that, but it requires that O.G. type honesty with yourself. What worked last year might demand a different approach today. Always be a teachable dog, respectfully. Decide to stay in the flow of traffic before you run out of road.

CHAPTER 8:
Get Their Attention
(DMs)

I remember, back in the 90s, when you would hear stories of artists being discovered in the most obscure places. It might be in a shopping mall, a subway, or a local hole-in-the-wall club, in a random unknown town. I often fantasized about being discovered in a similar fashion. My first rhyme partners, D.A., King Spry, along with Double R and I, would go to Tyrone Mall and, literally, walk up and down the aisles, rapping and singing our songs out loud, hoping that someone important would notice us! It's kind of funny when I think about it now, but we were convinced that if the right person heard us, they would instantly want to sign us to their label. We knew we were the best in our city, but we needed the world to know it.

The days of discovering talent in this way are long gone. Being in the right place at the right time still exists, but you're setting yourself up for disappointment if this is your plan to get put on. You must put in the legwork. There must be a budget in place for marketing and promotion. Artist Development is basically non-existent in today's industry. Before any of the movers and shakers will even consider dealing with you on a professional level, you must have a following already established.

While all these things are true, I still believe relationships are the cornerstone for success. With a good relationship comes positive communication, trust, support and favor. I understand when doing business there is a separation from the personal component. "It's just business, nothing personal" is a line we've all heard before in movies and TV. You must be extremely cautious when you mix the two, but we are humans first. I'm a person and you're a person,

45

before we ever decide to do business together. There is nothing quite like human connection. It's a phenomenon to be able to relate to and feel someone's joy, pain, love, suffering and to experience their heart. The comfort of a hug or the warmth of a kiss could, instantly, change the trajectory of a person's day.

I wanted to tap into that reality when I wrote "DMs." There is a line in the first verse when I say, "Mama, if they only knew the way your son destroys mics!" If the powers that be realized how special I am as an artist, they would not hesitate to give me an opportunity. This song is a modern-day fantasy of getting discovered by "sliding into the DMs" of someone who could change your life. It's my own version of "Please Listen To My Demo" by EPMD, who I refer to in the second verse. Really, it's an "imagine if" type of story.

Now, I'm not delusional by any stretch of the imagination. I understand these industry cats are very busy people and their inboxes are flooded with messages like mine. It is impossible to respond to every request they receive. They don't have the time to filter through all the coal, in hopes of finding the next diamond. But, what if one day they decided to click the link I shared in their inbox? I wonder if they'd be able to hear my heart. Would the skill level and my passion transfer through the digital distance between us?

I have witnessed with my own eyes and ears how my music has inspired others. I've seen grown men cry after listening to my lyrics. These labels have no idea of how lucrative it would be to have both a business and personal relationship with me. I don't say this to be cocky, but you must know what you bring to the table and how greatly others can benefit from what you have to offer. My belief that I was chosen to be able to inspire millions has never wavered. I felt that way as a kid, rapping in the mall, and I feel the same way today!

I say this because I've experienced this fantasy turn into reality in my own life before. I'm a huge fan of the Dungeon Family, out of Atlanta, GA, the music collective that brought us Outkast, Goodie Mob, Big Rube and Killer Mike. As a fellow Southern artist, their music really speaks to me because I speak their language. They also remind me a lot of my cousins, who live in Georgia, with their Southern drawl, not to mention the fact that they are extremely dope artists. A few years back I decided I wanted to "get their attention," so I uploaded a video of myself to Instagram, performing a 16-bar freestyle, where I included a bevy of Dungeon Family references. My intention was to convey that I was, indeed, a die-hard fan of their collective, but also to showcase my own ability to get busy with the rhymes. I tagged several members from their crew and I went about my day.

After a couple of hours passed, Khujo Goodie, of the Goodie Mob, not only "liked" but he shared my post on his page as well! I couldn't believe one of my musical heroes was now familiar with my work. The comments on his post were flooded with fire emojis. Fast forward a year and now Khujo was putting together a mixtape to shine the spotlight on unsigned independent artists. I submitted one of my songs for consideration and it got picked! "Two for two," I thought to myself.

Since that first video I posted, I've had Khujo on as a guest for my podcast, *SLIDES,* and more recently, he had me escorted backstage to meet the rest of the Goodie Mob when he spotted me in the front row at one of their concerts in Tampa, FL. He's a very humble human being, who isn't afraid to share industry advice with me from time to time. Khujo took a chance on me when I shared that video, and that chance allowed us to form a solid relationship. I set out to get the attention of some legends and that's precisely what I received.

Prior to meeting Khujo, I met another member of the Dungeon Family named Big Rube. If you're up on your knowledge of this legendary collective, then you know Big Rube is the burly voice behind the signature spoken word pieces on plenty of Outkast and Goodie Mob songs. Since I follow him on IG, I was alerted when he posted about possibly having him "guest feature" on your song. I figured I would shoot my shot, so I sent him an email and included my phone contact info, just in case. When I got a call back the next day, I was borderline in disbelief, upon hearing his iconic and distinctive voice on the other line.

After the initial excitement settled, we talked and bounced ideas back and forth about the interlude I wanted him to do for my album, *AUX Tales.* He left with a better understanding of who I was as an artist, and two months later he was on my album! All it took was a conversation. He could have been like, "I don't have time for this unknown dude from St. Petersburg, F.L." After all, he's collaborated with a who's who list of rappers and singers before me but, nevertheless, he was willing to connect. What's even more special is the fact that he charged me less the second time I worked with him than he did for the first song. He wanted to give me a deal because, as he put it, we worked well together, and he really enjoyed doing that initial interlude.

He once told me that he wished he had recorded that song for his album. It's kind of crazy when I think about it because I produced the music for the interlude about 4 years before I ever met Big Rube. I made it for me to rap to, but it was so different that I shelved it in hopes that one day the right artist would be paired with it to make it pop the way that it should. Big Rube was the perfect candidate and the only voice that made sense to speak over that track. Like Khujo, Rube and I talk from time to time. I'll send him music to preview, prior to me releasing it for the masses. Relationships go far beyond the business.

How do you get the right person's attention in a very busy world? You could have a gimmick, but I'm not fond of those. Gimmicks lack authenticity and lasting power. I believe the answer to the question is creativity. You must do something that sticks out from the crowd. I think back on the car that I won. Each participant was given the same instructions for writing the jingle. Knowing that there would be hundreds, if not thousands, of submissions, I had to come up with a creative idea that no one else would think of. Hmm, the car is called Kia Rio, right? Well, "Kia" is a girl's name, so what if I talked about the car like I was talking about a girl? When that thought entered my mind, I immediately relayed it to my wife and her response was "Don't you tell anybody else!" She knew it was a great idea from the onset.

I also thought that I should go above and beyond the criteria required, which was to name the same 5 features about the car. I went online and researched everything I could about this new vehicle. I was the only participant to include more features than what they asked for, and when I sat down with the dealers after winning the car, they made it a point to highlight that very fact. Being creative and going above the bare minimum will set you apart from the competition.

There is a unique theme recurring all throughout this "DMs" song that I won't reveal in this book. I don't want to spoil it for you, so you're going to have to listen to the song for yourself. The beat was made by the Ukranian producer, Svgar. I love his production style and the way he frequently utilizes the Spanish guitar. There is a mysterious, yet innocent element that attracted me to this composition. It conjured up feelings of a deep yearning when I heard it. As a writer, you never can predict the direction certain music will take you in, and that is what excites me. I allow the music and the Spirit of God to dictate what I write. What story are the instruments trying to assist in telling?

I was reminded of that young kid in Tyrone Mall, who wanted the world to know just how good he was. Just let me show you what I can do, and I promise you won't be disappointed. To add emphasis to the fact I wanted to get your attention, I asked the recording engineer to add a filtered effect to my vocal track. Usually, for uniformity purposes, I don't alter the effects on my voice, from track to track, but there are times when you must break the monotony to grab the listener's ear. I already possess a big booming voice but imagine that voice coming through a bullhorn. A sound like that will surely turn a few heads. I was well pleased with the result as the effect pierced through the production just as I suspected it would.

I wrote a melodic hook that I decided to sing myself. Normally, when I write anything with a melody, I'll have an actual singer perform it because my singing voice is... well let's just say Boyz II Men won't be calling me anytime soon! I wanted to sing this hook, however, because it was important for whoever the recipient was on the other end of that DM to, personally, hear my heart. I surprised myself, as it came out much better than I had anticipated.

If you want to be heard, then get creative. Don't just think outside of the box; think outside of the warehouse that the box is in! There is a Big Rube and a Khujo Goodie waiting to hear your voice. Grab your bullhorn and let them know that you exist!

49

CHAPTER 9:
Proverbs 18:22
(My Suga)

Two of my all-time favorite bible verses are found right next to one another. The first one is "Death and life *are* in the power of the tongue, And those who love it will eat its fruit." (Proverbs 18:21, New King James Version). My dad used to say, "The man who says he can and the man who says he can't are both right." Knowing this truth, I try to be very careful with the words that come out of my mouth. The second verse is "He *who* finds a wife finds a good *thing*, And obtains favor from the Lord" (Proverbs 18:22, New King James Version.)

Back in 1997, I found, not just a good, but a great thing! As I'm writing this, it dawned on me that I'm just two days shy of the 27-year anniversary of the date I met my lovely wife. I could have never imagined that nearly 30 years later, I would still be madly in love with this incredible woman. Here we are, 3 adult children and 1 adorable grandchild later. I've lost count of the number of songs I've written about her, but I never tire of doing so. She continues to inspire me, and I've obtained an insurmountable measure of favor by having her as my queen. It's impossible to quantify the impact of her presence in my life. She is my best friend, my prayer partner, my lover and so much more. The wonderful thing about marriage is that you're in a constant state of "learning" your spouse. Over the years, your partner's wants, likes and concerns will most likely change, so there is a level of adaptability that each person must possess if the marriage is to remain successful. Fortunately, our partnership began with a solid foundation. Marriage was instituted by God, and our union is a covenant between us and Him. He said that "It's not good for man to be alone," so He made him a helpmate. My wife is the epitome of that. I've grown in so many ways, and my wife is largely responsible for that growth. She challenges me to be the best version of myself possible. I know she'll tell me the truth, as opposed to what I want to hear, and I'm grateful for her honesty.

I remember when I first told my parents that I wanted to marry my wife. My dad asked how I knew she was the one, and I told him although I hadn't experienced a lot in life, I wanted to experience new things with her. That remains true to this day. We have experienced so much life together; parenthood, travel, weddings, funerals, promotion, job loss, joy, pain, breakups to makeups, we've seen it all. Through and through, Tonya Harrell has been right by my side.

Watching her operate as a mother is such a great joy. She's a natural. Caring, loving and very protective, she's always putting our children's needs before her own. She prays, non-stop, for our kids and our granddaughter, Athens. She's also a powerful woman of God, who's very active in our church. My point is, she's all that and a bag of Sweet Chili Doritos!

I remember the first time I spit a verse for her. We were in the car and I was playing an instrumental, produced by my brother, Black Speed. I had recently written a song called *"Déjà vu"* to it. It was one of those storytelling-type joints about a guy randomly meeting a beautiful woman out in public. I can't recall all the words, but I do remember the part where I said, *"I bussed a U-turn and I gave her a holler, I'm about to catch the bus, well, let me save you a dollar."* We had only known each other for about two months, so, of course, I was trying to impress her with my wordplay. She loved the verse so much that, later that day, she asked me to repeat the verse for her mother upon meeting her for the first time! I never forgot that moment, and it's probably the reason I enjoy writing songs about her, even to this day.

"My Suga" is a sincere and light-hearted ode to the woman of my dreams. This is the first song I wrote and recorded on the album. I had recently laid down a verse on my homie Theo Lane's song. I assume he was extremely grateful for my contribution because, shortly afterwards, he told me he was going to executive produce a song for me to use, however I saw fit. He said he would pick out and purchase a beat from the same producer who made the beat for the song he featured me on. Not only would he cop the beat, but he would also pay for the studio time to record the song. All he wanted in exchange was for me to return the favor and feature him on this song. I thought to myself, "Wow, this is a no-brainer!" I'm so thankful for my brother's kindness because this type of generosity doesn't happen every day.

When I got the beat, which was produced by Troi Dickey, I immediately fell in love with it. It sounded like a love song to me. The rhythm guitar had this groove that felt like the early-to-mid 90's. The horns on the hook were so jazzy. This instrumental sounded like it was designed, specifically, to be played at *The Sanctuary*, the infamous nightclub from the movie, *Love Jones*. I could visualize Darius and Nina, dancing skin to skin to this soul music.

The first thing I wanted to do was write a hook for Theo to sing. At this point, writing raps is something I can do in my sleep. What excites me, creatively speaking, is writing something melodic for another artist to perform. It helps if you're familiar with the artist that you are writing for. What type of voice do they have? How comfortable are they with different phrasings? What subjects resonate with them and fit their personality? Knowing Theo is a natural soul singer, I wanted to present this side of him and allow it to be the driving force of the song.

Sometimes, less *is* truly more. As a songwriter, there is always the possibility of over-writing and using more words than necessary. Your hook should be easy to learn, repeat and sing along to. I thought, "What if he just repeats the words 'My Suga' multiple times for the chorus?" If he used different inflections each time he sang it, that just might do the trick. It didn't take long for me to allow the chord progression to dictate where I should go with it. It's hard to explain, but sometimes it feels as if these songs simply write themselves.

Once I was satisfied with what I wrote, I sent Theo a voice memo of me singing the hook to see how he liked it. In true Theo fashion, he hit me back and said, "That's hot, Shad!" I was glad he liked it, but it still felt like it was missing something. I didn't want the hook to be static, so I decided to rap on the second half, in between Theo's lines. This helped prevent the chorus from becoming too repetitive, and it gave it some motion, so to speak.

Me being the acronym lover that I am, chose to create one for the word 'Suga." I'm also a bit of an overachiever, so why stop at just one meaning? I love a good challenge, so I decided to come up with 4 different acronyms for "Suga": (1) Sweet Unique Godly Angel, (2) who takes Selfies Using Good Angles, (3) she Shows Up like she's Got an Appointment, and (4) She's Undeniably God's Anointed.

Now that the hook was both Theo and Shad approved, I proceeded to pen my verses. Following the theme of "My Suga" I figured it would be dope to start multiple lines out with that phrase, explaining who "My Suga" is exactly. I wanted to show the many facets of my lovely wife. She's creative, loving, smart and funny. She's a woman of God and so much more! Whereas some songs on the album are heavily influenced by our relationship, "My Suga" is a direct dedication to my wife.

When I first received the track, it did not include a bassline. As soulful as it was, it needed that extra umph to bring it all the way home. Thankfully, being part of a band has its perks. I reached out to my bass player from The Real Clash, Seany D., to see if he would lay down a bassline for the song. I gave him free reign to create a groove of his own.

Often, I'll hear the music in my head, as I'm writing, and I'll hum it out and record it to my phone. Then I send that recording to my musician friends to flesh it out with their instruments. I've written more songs than I can remember using this method, but I fell back this time to see where Sean would take the track. He did not disappoint!

I was more than pleased when he sent the track back with the new bassline included. It sounded playful, innocent and soulful, all at the same time. It complemented what Troi had already created in such a great way. The drums and bass are the rhythm section of a song. The drums serve as the heartbeat of the song, while the bass gives the song its soul. Usually when a producer composes, these are the first two instruments he or she will utilize. This makes what Seany D. did that much more impressive, because the bass was the final instrument added. The song would not be the same without it.

This is one of my wife's favorite songs I've written so far. Now, I know you're probably thinking, "Of course it's her favorite because it's about her!" Remember when I mentioned, earlier, that she tells me the truth, not what I want to hear? There have been times where she was completely not feeling my music, even if the song was about her. Maybe the beat didn't go with the words or my flow wasn't catchy enough but, whatever the case, she always gives her honest opinion.

Selfishly, I want her to pull out her pom-poms every time I show her new material, but that isn't always the case. I've developed some tough skin and I respect her opinion, even if I disagree. As artists, like Erykah Badu once famously said, we are sensitive about our music. I've learned to not get offended. In fact, I use her as a measuring stick on how well the music might be received by others. She has a knack for recognizing a hit song when she hears it. Although art is subjective, some songs just have that "it-factor" so, as an artist, you want to be open to constructive criticism, when you present your work for public consumption. I often think, if my wife likes it, that's a good indicator I'm on to something. Even if the song is not about her, I believe, subconsciously, I'm hoping to get that same reaction I got from her the first time I rapped for her!

My wife is a walking miracle. She overcame two strokes in June of 2022, with zero residual effects. I won't go into too much detail, as she will elaborate and give her testimony in her upcoming book, but just know she's a fighter and I am blessed to be her husband.

The last point I'd like to make about my Suga is her ability to make me laugh. We are both goofy and silly at times, which makes for a fun marriage. She can crack on the way I walk, while I tease her about confidently mispronouncing certain words, but it's all love at the end of the day. Laughter truly is medicine for the soul. My wife keeps me spiritually medicated daily, so it's only right I continue to pen my adoration for her. God blessed me with a good thing when I found "My Suga."

CHAPTER 10:
Imagination Unlocked
(Locs)

Perhaps the most important item in a songwriter's toolbox is a powerful imagination. Witty ideas, groundbreaking inventions, solutions to problems and inspirational stories all lie in an invisible realm known as our imagination. Just stop and think about it for a moment. Every single invention known to man, first began as a thought in someone's head. The houses that we live in, the roads on which we drive, even this book that you're reading, started as an idea. The bigger your imagination, the more interesting your stories become.

I'm a sucker for a good, animated film. If I'm channel surfing and I stumble across *Shrek* or *Finding Nemo,* I'm parking it right there. Instantly, I'm transported into their worlds. I feel like I'm right there with Shrek and Donkey, on an adventure to a land, far, far away. I'm swimming along with Marlin and Dory, searching frantically to rescue poor little Nemo. The vibrant colors of the movie serve as visual stimuli. The graphics and movements of the characters are simply mind-blowing. The presentation is so well executed that, for the next hour and a half, I forget that the voices of the animated characters are coming from actual human beings. I've teleported from reality to fantasy in a matter of seconds! And to think, what I'm watching started out as an unseeable thought in someone's brain.

Often, reality can be a scary place. A great movie, or song, can help us, momentarily, escape the harshness of what is real. Imagination offers possibilities. What if? What if things were like *this* instead? What if I made this decision instead of that one?

Since I was a little kid, I've had a huge imagination. I wondered what it would be like to be as strong as my favorite super-hero, The Incredible Hulk. I wanted to know what Prince Adam felt like the moment he transformed into He-Man. It makes sense why I became a rapper when I think about it.

My parents named me Rashad. I always liked that my name was different from everyone else's. It made me feel special. In fact, my dad once told me that I would never find an older "Rashad" than myself. I was named after the NFL great, Ahmad Rashad. My parents liked the name "Rashad," but they had never heard it used as a first name. I don't know how true my dad's words were, but, to this day, every "Rashad" I've ever met was younger than me.

As cool as my name is, I wanted to use a different rapper name. I wanted an identity that was separate from "Rashad." Blame it on comic books and cartoons, but I needed an alter-ego – someone who possessed a superpower! So, at 16 years of age, I created "Shadcore." Sometimes, "Rashad" can be a bit unsure of himself, but "Shadcore" is loud, boisterous and full of confidence. If you hand "Shadcore" a microphone, or a pen and a pad, the ground begins to shake. Lightning strikes, as his muscles enlarge, causing his jeans to split at the seams, and his skin morphs from mocha brown to gamma ray green!

I'll never forget when my parents came to see me and my group, BRUTAL FUNK, perform in a talent show back in 1995. As we were exiting the stage, my dad walked up with a huge grin on his face. He said, "Son, you completely transformed when you were on that stage! That was incredible!" What my dad was witnessing was the metamorphosis of "Rashad" to "Shadcore."

When I'm in the creative process, my imagination is always on "go." You never know where the beat is going to take you when you first hear it. The possibilities are endless. This part of songwriting is always enjoyable for me. Your mind begins to race all over the place, in search of a concept or subject matter that will fit like a glove with the music. I often ask myself, "what is the music trying to convey? What words are dying to be said over this production? What is the theme? How does the track make me feel?"

The beat for "Locs" was so crazy to me, when I heard it for the first time. To say it was "different" would be an understatement. "This Ukrainian producer just keeps pulling trick after trick out of his bag!", I marveled. My favorite producer in the world is Timbaland, and this reminded me of something he would make. Svgar's signature Spanish guitar showed up to the party again, but in an entirely new and exciting way. The 808 is so profound on this track. It's the star of the show. The way he made it sound like it "fell down a flight of stairs," once every 8 bars, was pure genius! This beat is insane! It's bouncy and very youthful.

I began to mumble, rhythmically, to the beat, while listening in my bedroom. No words were formulated. I was strictly focusing on rhythm, flow and cadence. I couldn't stop bobbing and shaking my head. I remember, briefly thinking to myself, "This sounds like something young kids with dreads would shake their hair to!" Then I started to imagine a dreadlocked artist, performing in front of thousands of dreadlocked fans over this beat.

It felt like the rap equivalent to the big hair rock bands of the '80s, when they'd vigorously shake their long hair, up and down, while shredding on their guitars. These images grew more and more prevalent with each listen. "If I had dreads, I'd shake 'em!", I humorously thought. I didn't realize it at the time, but the seed was already planted for the song's conceptual direction. I kept repeating "If I had dreads, I'd shake 'em!" over the music. Sure, it seemed like a silly concept, but I couldn't deny how catchy this developing hook was.

I thought to myself, "This is hip-hop and, as an emcee, I get to make up my own rules." Besides, there was a time when rap songs used to be more light-hearted. Will Smith, or should I say The Fresh Prince, wrote a song called "I Think I Can Beat Mike Tyson." Sir Mix-A-Lot made "Buttermilk Biscuits." I continued to craft the hook, until the flow and the lyrics were right where I wanted them.

Although I'm almost 50 years old, I'm a big fan of the Migos' flow. I put that disclaimer out there because there is a false narrative in Hip-Hop culture that suggests the older guys don't like the younger ones and vice versa. While this "get off my lawn" mentality may be true for some of my peers, it doesn't speak for us all. I'm fascinated with the way the artform continues to evolve. Over time, fashion, flow and the familiar all will inevitably change. Sometimes for the good, and other times, not so much. What particularly wows me is the way the flow changes, from generation to generation. The way rappers are *still* discovering new pockets to flow in is mind-boggling.

Even though it's clear that the Migos were influenced by their elders, Bone Thugs & Harmony in particular, they still found a way to make their music their own. I purposefully channeled that style for "Locs." My objective was to use my voice as a percussive instrument, rhythmically complementing the beat with a ferocious and deliberate triplet flow. Since the concept was very animated to begin with, I chose to stay on topic, during the verses, to further reiterate the point. If I did have a head full of dreads, I'd shake them, non-stop, because the music energizes me in that way. So, that's what I talked about the entire time.

My imagination allowed me to see myself as a young, energetic, dreadlocked emcee, performing in front of a sold-out Coachella crowd. I might be an older, bald, fat dude, but when "Locs" comes on, I turn into Offset, and I commence to "set it off"! That's the power of the imagination.

I love previewing new music I record with my children, so when I let my daughter, Tasanee, hear this for the first time, I asked her what the song should be called. Right away, she said "Locs." I thought about it for a second and I said, "You know what? I like it!" It's straight to the point, plus it's a one-syllable word. I love one-syllable song titles.

In the final verse, I have a line where I say, "I could never fit in no box." I know that isn't proper English, but you get my drift. My imagination is too large to box in. As an artist, I can express myself in a myriad of ways. One day, I might write something that'll make you cry, and the next day, my words could have you literally laughing out loud! These are the attributes that make for a great album. You want to have a well-balanced variety of feelings, vibes, concepts and straight up bangers, when you present a body of work.

It's been my experience that artists who follow this formula resonate the most with their listeners. I want you to have a human experience when you listen to my music. Somedays, we feel like crying. Somedays, we want to chill. Maybe, today, you're feeling adventurous. My job is to provide the soundtrack for these different feelings, even if it means going to a land far, far away just to shake your invisible dreads!

CHAPTER 11:
The Beauty of Collaboration
(Grey Gucci Shades)

To make a great album requires a healthy dose of variety. You have to include different moods, various tempos and diverse subject matter. Every song doesn't need to necessarily be "deep". Sometimes you just need something to vibe to and that's where "Grey Gucci Shades" comes in. This is "30 MPH and under music." You marinate in this type of song, while enjoying the ear candy of the multiple voices and the intriguing instrumentation.

As a songwriter, there's always an obvious intentionality present, but one should also be open to spontaneity. Allow the music to dictate the direction you go in. Never force the issue. When I received this beat from 1Weeley, another cold email producer, it sounded like "vibe" music. I could, immediately, hear my sister Eliana B.'s voice floating all over this. The way the guitar wails, just once, every four bars, is sonically stimulating. The 808s are placed and spaced out enough to allow the track to breathe, which gives room for the words to stand out, even more.

"Grey Gucci Shades" went through several phases to become what it ended up being. I knew I wanted to share this space with Eliana, because her voice was tailor-made for this type of production. With that in mind, I began to imagine exactly what she would sing about over this track. The music was reminiscent of "Aston Martin Music" by Rick Ross, so I wanted Eliana to play Chrisette Michele to my Rozay! The first line Chrisette sings in the hook is "vibin' to the music." I decided that this would be the overarching theme for my song. It was important for the listener to catch a "vibe" when they heard this.

60

Let me just say this before I go on. I never tire of hearing Eliana sing the words I write. It's like I provide her with a skeleton, while her voice gives the bones its flesh and breath. She then adds her heart and soul to make the words come alive! I built the hook around the word "vibe." "Fly is too basic a word to describe your style, let's vibe a while," I wrote. I didn't even have a working concept for the song, yet, until I came up with that line.

This is what I meant about being spontaneous as a songwriter. The creative process isn't always linear. Sometimes you write without a subject matter being fully hashed out. Even the song title might come later down the road. Follow your instincts and don't allow "overthinking" to stagnate your progress.

Once I had the first line of the hook, the concept for my verse came to me right away. I imagined it was a beautiful, sunny day in Tampa Bay, Florida. I saw a group of guys, walking on the beach, each rocking a pair of sunglasses, as they approached an oncoming group of women. There was an instant attraction between a male and female member from both groups. Now, typically in these situations, the guy would make the first move, but since he was so undeniably "fly," she decided to step to him instead. Can you tell that a man wrote this song?

So, I had a working concept and the first line of the chorus, up to this point. Before I finished writing my rap verse, I wanted to complete the hook: "*High as a Pterodactyl, I wanna go where I've never travelled. You lift my feet right off the gravel. I'm taking flight with you!*" This is what I pictured the young lady saying to the guy. She's so attracted to his style and his overall vibe that she, literally, wants to go wherever he is going. I mentioned how all the guys were wearing sunglasses, and this is what gave me the inspiration for the title, "Grey Gucci Shades."

I began to think about the type of sunglasses these men were wearing. I figured they couldn't be sporting some regular cheap shades if they were going to arrest the attention of these women. They had to be rocking something fancy and upscale to match the words Eliana was singing about. Something expensive and designer would be ideal. Gucci shades popped in my mind. That was a good start, but I needed something a little more descriptive. To make it distinct, I added a color. Let's make the shades grey and call it "Grey

Gucci Shades." Yeah, I like that. It's got a ring to it, plus I love alliteration. The song title also creates a natural curiosity that a generic title just wouldn't provide.

See, this is what the creative process looks like. One thought or idea leads to the next, and so on and so forth. I didn't think of the chorus all at one time. I thought of one line and that line led me to the song's concept. Once I knew where I wanted to go with it, I was able to complete the hook. The completion of the hook then led to the title of the song. Rarely do you get the full picture up front. Much like a painting, the masterpiece slowly reveals itself, as you add lines and color to the canvas.

So, I had the title, the first verse and the hook completed when I noticed something. My point had already been made during my verse and there was nowhere else for me, personally, to go with it, so I thought it would be a good idea to feature another emcee on the song with me. I started going through my mental Rolodex, imagining what artist would complement this beat the most.

My homie, Charli Funk, immediately came to mind. He's got the best flow of all the artists I've ever worked with. His ability to flow in different pockets of the beat is unmatched. I once said to him, "I don't know if this is a real word, but your flow is so metronomic!" He's got very clear diction, (not to mention he sounds a lot like Andre 3000), so I figured he'd be the perfect addition to this song. I reached out to see if he was down to collaborate and, of course, he said "Let's do it!"

We set a date to record the song. It was going to be a tight window for Charli to make it, because he was scheduled to work that day, but the appointment time was during his lunch break. I arrived at the studio and, quickly, laid my verse down. Eliana came in shortly after and did her part. Charli, however, was unable to get there during his break, so we couldn't complete the song that day.

Unfortunately, this meant I had to reschedule for a later date, which basically equaled more money. I like to get a song recorded and finished on the same day because studio costs are expensive to begin with. The plan was to come back later for Charli to record his verse, but we kept having scheduling conflicts. He and I both are extremely busy men, and since this song wasn't designated for an album, at the time, I decided to put it on the back burner. For the next ten months, it collected digital dust.

One day, my group, KRK, and I were discussing the need to add more songs to our limited catalog. I remembered "Grey Gucci Shades" was still unfinished. I told the guys about the song and how I wanted to feature Charli Funk on it, but we never got around to it. "We can make this a KRK song, and still feature Eliana and Charli Funk on it if y'all are cool with it," I proposed. Theo and O.G. were both down with the idea and I was glad to know that we'd finally get to finish this dope song.

The plan was for O.G. to rhyme second, Charli Funk third, and for Theo to do some ad libs throughout the entire song. We set a date and this time Charli Funk was in attendance! It was a great experience, having all three of my brothers in the studio at the same time, as this would be the first time Charli got to meet O.G. and Theo.

I love that I was blessed with countless opportunities to introduce so many of my music friends to one another. Whether it's Theo and O.G., Troy and Eliana, O.G. and J. Ack, or a combination of them all, it brings me joy to know I played a role in helping to establish these relationships. I champion the idea of collaboration. I never try to keep my resources to myself. I'm a fan of dope music, so if I can put a couple of dope strangers in a room together to make something dope, then that's a win for us all! Many of these artists have gone on to form lasting bonds, outside of music, and that is a beautiful thing.

On O.G. 's verse, he creates a similar scenario to mine, except his setting takes place on International Drive, in Orlando, instead of the beach. He's feeling good about himself, as he sparks up a conversation with a heart-dropping cutie, who finds his dialect to be very intriguing. Normally, O.G. is an in-your-face, aggressive emcee, but I love the fact that he knew how to dial it back for this song. He sounds smooth, calm and collected, with a quiet confidence, which women find incredibly attractive. My brother definitely understood the assignment!

Here's why the song ended up on my album, instead of KRK's. We never found a spot where Theo could truly be showcased up front. We considered having him sing along with Eliana on the chorus, but it didn't make sense to say the same words that she was saying. The hook was intended to come from a woman's perspective, so we scrapped that idea. We also thought about him having his own verse, but that would have made the song entirely too long.

We didn't want to cheat Theo's fanbase, or our own, by making it a KRK song, where Theo is hardly featured, so I decided to turn it back into a Shadcore song. I knew I would feature Theo elsewhere on my album, so it was okay if he hung out in the background on this one. He adds just enough variety and flavor to the mix, complementing Eliana's vocals, while she takes lead. This is another reason why I said the song went through many phases to become what it became.

Here's a fun fact. I never heard Charli Funk's verse, until we recorded it that day! So, for about a year, I didn't know what he was going to talk about. If I ask someone to be on a song with me, it means I trust their pen, so I don't necessarily need to hear their verse prior to the recording session. Plus, I know that they know what I'm going to bring to the table, therefore they're automatically going to elevate their game, making for a dope song.

While O.G. chose to go in a similar direction as I did, highlighting the initial attraction between a man and a woman, Charli Funk's GPS took him to an entirely different location. He opted to address ideas of unification and ignoring your haters. At first listen, it may appear a bit off topic but, strangely enough, it works! Remember, earlier I said the overarching theme of the song was "vibin' to the music," and the importance of allowing the music to dictate what you write about? Well, this is where the music took Charli, and I'm glad it did, because it breaks up the monotony, yet keeps it interesting. He adds an additional 8 bars, which puts an exclamation point on a well-crafted masterpiece.

I catch a vibe every time I listen to this song. Our lyrics are so bright and vivid that it requires a special kind of eyewear to avoid potential blindness. I strongly suggest that you grab a pair of grey Gucci shades, so you can vibe along with us!

CHAPTER 12:
A Rich Culture
(My Favorite Color)

In October of 2023, I gave myself a bold challenge. I don't even know what motivated this decision, but I pushed myself to see it through, all the way to the end. For the entire month, I challenged myself to write a new 16 bar verse, every day! 16 bars were the bare minimum. Some days, I wrote 24 bars. Other days, I wrote as many as 40. My goal was to sharpen my skills and to be proactive with the pen, as opposed to waiting for inspiration to strike.

Just imagine that for a moment. I've already been rapping since I was nine years old, yet here I was, knowing I still had room for improvement. So, every day, I'd either write a verse on paper, my phone, or on many occasions, both. I made voice memos daily and sent them to a few friends, as a way of holding myself accountable. I should also add that most of the verses were written without a beat. I say that because, typically, songs are written to music and not the other way around. However, I've been rapping for so long that I can write to an imaginary beat in my head if I must. I'm proud to say by the end of that October, I had completed 31 new verses!

On one of those days, I remember sending a voice memo of my verse to my brother, Double R. He was there from the beginning, so I knew he could appreciate how far I had come on this journey. When he heard what I sent him, his response was, "Please tell me you're going to make a song out of this?" My intentions for doing this exercise weren't necessarily to make actual songs, but more so to get better as an overall writer. However, Double R's reaction to this verse grabbed my attention. I took his advice and turned the first verse of "My Favorite Color" into a whole song!

When I wrote that initial verse during the 31-Day Challenge, it started out as somewhat of a humorous joke. I was thinking about some funny things that are synonymous with "Black culture" in America. "How many ways can I express my Blackness in 16 bars?" I imagined. What began as pure comedy ended up becoming so much more. As I was writing these various expressions of Black culture, there was a deep awareness unraveling of the responsibility to showcase the complexities of Black life in America. I couldn't talk only about the funny stuff. I had to address some serious issues, as well. Weaving in and out of humor, honesty and healing became my main objective.

As a people, we are certainly not a monolith, but there are some similarities that only we share, and that's what I wanted to focus on. Our culture is a culture that I'm extremely proud to be a part of. This is a song about self-appreciation. It's about self-love and being comfortable in the beautiful skin that you're in

The content is so layered that it's difficult to know where to begin, but let's start here. Years ago, I was made privy of the "doll test." This was a series of experiments, conducted by Kenneth and Mamie Clark, back in the 1940s. The purpose of these experiments was to study the psychological effects of segregation on Black children. What the Clarks would do is present four dolls that were identical (except for skin color) to a group of three- to seven-year-old Black children, and ask them questions like, "Which dolls are nice?" and "Which dolls are bad?", "Which dolls are pretty?" and "Which dolls are ugly?" Most of the kids preferred the white dolls. They said that the Black dolls were "bad" and that the white dolls looked most like them. (Naacpldf, n.d.)

It was concluded that discrimination, segregation and prejudice all were major contributors to Black children having low self-esteem and feeling inferior to whites. This research would prove to be vital in the landmark *Brown vs. Board of Education* case to advance integration into schools.

I was blown away when I learned of this test. It was also a stinging reminder that people went to great lengths to de-humanize us and make us feel less than. Sadly, we live in a day where folks would rather remove books from the schools that educate us on the history of slavery in this country, than to face the ugly truth about its devastating effects.

I'm so thankful that my parents raised me to know who I am. They taught me that I wasn't better, nor was I less than the next person. "Black is beautiful" is a phrase that we often heard growing up in the Harrell household. My sisters played with Black dolls. Our parents instilled a sense of pride in us. That's what I wanted to do with this song. I'm only one generation removed from segregated bathrooms and water fountains. Whether you learn about that in a classroom, or by reading this book, the truth is it happened. My parents lived it. I've heard some of the horror stories. As awful as it was, they overcame it. They taught me to be an overcomer, too. That's what I love about being Black – our ability to persevere, despite seemingly impossible circumstances.

Defeating obstacles and thriving against all odds is just one of the many layers. We are also the purveyors of "cool." We set a bevy of trends, from fashion and style to music and dance. Some of the world's most notable inventions were created by Black people.

Alexander Miles invented automatic elevator doors. The three-light traffic signal was created by a Black man named Garrett Morgan. He also created the gas mask! Frederick Jones made the thermostat. Phillip Downing invented the mailbox. The first home security system was created by a Black woman named Mary Van Brittan Brown. The list goes on and on.

Greatness is in our DNA. What this song does is the opposite of what those slaveowners were attempting to do – it humanizes us. We are real people with real emotions, feelings and ambitions. We want the best for our children, just like everybody else. Contrary to how we've historically been painted, we are *not* savages. We help shape American culture.

I wrote this entire song before I had a beat for it. I didn't know exactly what I wanted the music to sound like, but I knew it had to be special for a song of this magnitude. Sometimes, the marriage between the beat and the bars is so divine, you must accredit God for His participation in the matter! I was in the studio one day, working on a KRK song, with my brothers, Theo and O.G.

The producer of "My Favorite Color," Jay Wiz, was showing O.G. some of his beats for O.G. to potentially use for his solo album.

He played the "My Favorite Color" beat and I immediately started spittin' the verse I had shown Double R a few weeks prior! I was not about to let O.G. get any bright ideas. I knew right away that this was the beat I had been waiting on for this song. I hated to impose but I had to. Thankfully, O.G. liked what he heard, and he agreed that the music fit perfectly to what I was saying. In fact, it was O.G. who called me later that day and insisted I put a deposit down on the beat, to secure it before Jay Wiz played it for someone else. I was glad he conceded.

We had a similar situation happen a few years prior to this one. We were in the studio with our brother, Troy Cedeño, as he was showing us some of his latest work. He previewed a track that made both O.G. and myself sit up straight! O.G. told Troy he was willing to pay for the beat, right there on the spot. If this were a game of spades, O.G. had just thrown out the big Joker! There was nothing I could do, because like Rakim once said, "digging in my pockets, I was still coming up with lint." My boy O.G. is a real one though, because he offered me a guest spot to hop on the song with him. Of course, I said "yes," and we ended up recording one of our best tracks yet, "Go Papi," which is featured on O.G.'s album, *Never Quit*.

My attraction to the "My Favorite Color" track was the Wakanda-like chants, over the Africa-Meets-The-Trap drums. It's hard to describe, but the beat sounded "Black" to me. It prompted me to spit that specific verse, due to its ethnic sound. The way Jay Wiz was bobbing his head, as I rapped over his beat, was proof positive this music and my words belonged together.

The horns, originally, were placed earlier in the track, during the verse, but I thought they were better served for the hook only. I kept the instrumentation on the verses as sparse as possible, so that the words could really cut through. Saving the horns for the hook made that section hit that much harder, in my opinion. The chorus is a gut-punch that makes no apologies, whatsoever. It's a reminder for anyone who thought we might one day fade away, that we are, indeed, here to stay, forever.

We added one final piece to solidify this banger, right before we ended the session. James, the sound engineer, asked if I wanted to do anything else before we moved on. I liked what was going on in the intro, with the percussion, but it seemed kind of empty and bare by itself. I thought it could benefit by having a quote or soundbyte about "Blackness" at the beginning, to help set up my verse.

We both went to YouTube, on our phones, and began searching for "famous Black quotes." Before we knew it, a Dave Chappelle clip popped up from his legendary comedy special, *Killing Me Softly*. I knew, right away, that this was the snippet I would use. It had just the right amount of humor to go along with all the colloquialisms I was about to spew out. I also figured, since I opened the song with comedy, I'd close it in the same fashion. So, Chappelle opens *and* closes the song.

For as long as I can remember, the word "Black" has had a negative connotation. Black widow, Black Plague and black cats bring bad luck, just to name a few. Black is mysterious. I'm sure for any non-Black person, there *is* a certain mystique to us. "How were they able to overcome centuries of oppression?" "How come they run so much faster than everyone else?" "How come they're so good at what they do?" "How come they seem to age backwards?" Black is beautiful. Black is powerful. Black represents greatness, and it just so happens to be my favorite color.

CHAPTER 13:

Mama

(Sweet Tea on Sundays)

"Band-aids for the cuts. Aloe for the burns. Robitussin for the colds. Mama's always concerned for her children" are the opening lines to "Sweet Tea on Sundays." Our mothers are natural problem-solvers. They provide solutions for our dilemmas. Where would we be without Mama? Standing at just 5 feet tall, my mother is a force to be reckoned with. To know her is to love her. She loves God and family, above all. I am so fortunate to be her son.

Growing up in our household, we could feel the love permeating through those walls. I'm the eldest of three. I have two sisters – April and Autumn. We were blessed to have both of our parents in the home to raise us. My heart always went out to my cousins who did not share that experience in their childhood. I felt guilty when I thought about my family members who didn't have their dads in the home with them. I thanked God for how strong their mothers were, despite the challenges of doing it all alone. It took for me to become a parent to realize how difficult it is to raise children with both parents present, let alone by yourself.

My dad worked the graveyard shift, at the Post Office, so most of his days were spent sleeping. Mama would make breakfast for us, or we'd fix ourselves a bowl of cereal, and off to school we went. She attended PTA meetings, as education was very important in our house. For years, she worked at Allstate, through the day, and when she got off, she continued her motherly duties. There was always a hot meal for dinner, and we all sat at the dinner table and ate together.

We, religiously, said our grace before digging in. *"Once again, we're glad to be joining hands as a family. May this food we share today help us grow in every way!"* Amen! We talked about anything and everything at dinner time. There weren't any cellphones to distract us, but Daddy made sure the TV was turned off, and we also didn't answer the housephone while we were having dinner. I didn't appreciate the structure back then, but as a parent, I do now.

When family members would spend the night, they'd see the way we live, and soon enough, they started calling us "The Huxtables," referencing the hit '80s show, *The Cosby Show*. This was not an act for us, though. This was our lifestyle, long before an episode of The Cosby Show ever aired.

While Daddy was the provider and the disciplinarian, Mama was the super glue. She was the nurturer. My mom has always been supportive of my music, as well. I remember when I'd show her some of my earlier recordings, she would say things like, "Son, it sounds good, but I can't understand what you're saying. You need to enunciate your words." That was some of the best advice I ever received. She also told me not to curse and not to degrade women. She said, "You have a mama, and you wouldn't want anyone to put her down, right?" I still follow that advice today. I always wanted to make my parents proud when it came to my music. Even with my dad being gone, I still try to honor him with my material.

My mother took me to my very first concert, back in 1983. The GAP Band, Zapp & Roger and Midnight Star were all on the same bill. We had so much fun, singing and dancing along to the very music I had already grown accustomed to hearing in the Florida Room. I was so worn out near the end of the show that I fell asleep during The GAP Band's set. Thankfully, I woke right up when they played my jam, "You Dropped a Bomb on Me!"

Fun fact: My mom saves EVERYTHING! Sometimes, when I'm at her house, she'll pull out old report cards and certificates I received back in elementary school. Everything is in pristine condition, too. Recently, she gave me the ticket stub from that very concert we attended in 1983! Can you believe that? That concert was over 40 years ago! I keep that stub in my wallet, as a reminder that it was the first concert I ever attended and that I got to experience that with my mom.

I've always been impressed with my mother's faith in God. She made sure that my sisters and I went to Sunday School and to church, every Sunday. There's a saying she used to say, back then, and she still says it today; "Give God some of your time. You've got time for everything else!"

My mom was raised, primarily, by her grandmother. Her mom was in her life, but she was a teen-mom, just 14-years-old when she had my mother. My mother's father never claimed her and, unfortunately, it remained that way until he passed a few years ago. I never had a chance to meet my grandfather.

She was raised in the church and, despite the absence of a father in her own life, she prayed that, one day, God would bless her with a man who was a great father and a loving husband. God answered that prayer and He's been answering prayers for my mom her whole life.

I mentioned before that she was (and still is) the glue to our family. Not just for my immediate family, but to my extended family, as well. She still organizes many of our get-togethers and events. Family means everything to my mom. It always has. Some of my cousins, on my dad's side, used to think that "Auntie Pat" was the blood relative, while my dad married into the family! That's just how close we've always been. If some of my family fell on hard times, mom was there to help get them back on their feet. I've shared my room on several occasions, with uncles and cousins, happy to lend a helping hand. Mama taught me how to be grateful for what I have, considerate of others and sensitive towards those who were less fortunate. By helping family, mom was doing God's work, offering compassion and love, just like Jesus does for us all.

Without question, my mother's biggest faith test was the loss of my father; her best friend and husband of 40 years. At the time, she was still grieving and processing the loss of her one and only baby sister, my Auntie Jackie, who passed 3 years prior to my dad. I can't imagine the pain of losing a spouse, but my mom had to endure that. My dad was her everything. How was she to go on with life, as she knew it, without her closest friend by her side? All she could do was rely on the love of God, to get her through it. Although she was deeply saddened and in serious emotional pain, she knew God would give her the strength to smile again.

72

In November of 2020, my mother caught Covid. It landed her in the hospital for a week. She developed pneumonia and it scared me tremendously. She was in that age range that was most at-risk to succumbing to this terrible disease. We prayed, fervently, for her to have a full recovery. I broke down in tears, a few times, at the thought of losing my mama. Her health ultimately improved and she walked out of that hospital with her faith still intact. This, however, was a reality check, for me, that one day this road will have to be crossed.

My mother often brings up Ecclesiastes, Chapter 3, where the author talks about "times and seasons." She's always saying, "Shad, there's a time for everything." I want to enjoy and celebrate my mother, while I still have her with me. She deserves to smell her flowers, and one of the best bouquets I can give her is a song! I get my love for writing and my creativity from her, so I wanted to give back and show my appreciation by writing "Sweet Tea on Sundays."

I call it that because that is one of my favorite activities to do throughout the week. As I stated earlier, my workload is super demanding. I work two jobs, both Monday till Friday, and I don't get to see family, outside of my household, as often as I'd like. On Sundays, I make sure to visit my mama after church. I've been doing this since my children were little babies.

My mom makes the best sweet tea on the planet! She usually has a full pitcher in the fridge when I come over. My sister, April, and I love the stuff! April likes to mix hers with lemonade but, I like mine straight, no chaser! We use this time to get caught up on the week and to enjoy each other's company. Sometimes, we'll sit at the dinner table and talk, and other times we'll go in the backyard so she can show me what fruits and vegetables she's growing. Recently, we made our own wine, using the muscadine grapes she grows every year. We continue to find new ways to bond, which is truly a blessing.

When I realized I wanted to write a tribute song for my mother, I knew the beat had to be fire! So, I figured, since my Ukrainian connection was on a great streak, I'd see if he had anything that I could use. I originally wrote it to a different beat, but I learned shortly afterwards that the beat I wanted had already been purchased by another artist. I patiently waited for him to send a new batch of possibilities.

About a week later, he sent a pack of 10 beats. Carefully, I sifted through each one, hoping to find the one that was just right. I came across one that was dripping with soul. It sounded like "Sunday afternoon" to me. This is it! I didn't even need to listen to the remaining beats in the email. Sometimes, you just "know".

After I wrote the hook, I was thinking about naming the song, "For You, Mama." It wasn't a bad title, but it wasn't specific, nor was it catchy enough for me. By now, you know I take these titles very seriously. I started thinking about the activities we enjoy doing together. I thought, "Well this song *sounds* like Sunday. Plus, I enjoy going to my mama's house to get a mason jar full of sweet tea on Sundays!" Voila! There it is. "Sweet Tea on Sundays." If no one else gets the title, she will, and that's all that matters.

It's hard to narrow down what someone so special means to you, in just 3 minutes, so I hit as many points as I could, and I left it at that. I mentioned specific things, like Thanksgiving dinners, a memory of her having lunch with me at my school when I was a 1st grader, what she meant to my dad, her faith in God, and her relationships with her grandkids and her great-granddaughter.

I knew I had something when I shared the song with O.G., and he said it was just as powerful and potent as "Dear Mama" by 2Pac! That's as high a compliment as one could get, considering "Dear Mama" is my favorite mama-tribute song of all-time. When Pac died, my mother noticed me listening to "Dear Mama" in my bedroom. She asked if this was the rapper who had just been shot. She sat and listened to the entire song and told me how much she enjoyed it. We shared a moment that day, as she could feel the pain that I was experiencing from losing one of the greatest, far too soon.

My mom also taught me not to give up. Back in 1994, I was working as a dishwasher. It was only my second time working a regular job. I had lost my job at Winn-Dixie, five months prior to landing a gig at Bennigan's Restaurant. After about a week's worth of training with the head-dishwasher, they decided to let me loose, on a busy Saturday night. Thinking I had everything under control, I took a 30-minute break, and upon my return, I found dishes piled to the ceiling! There was no way I could get caught up, by myself, and worse, no one was coming to rescue me. I was so overwhelmed that

I took off my soiled apron, threw my hat on the ground, and I walked out. I quit, right there, on the spot.

The next day, my mama asked why I wasn't at work, when she saw I was still at the crib. I said, "I quit, Ma. It was too much." My mother told me to go back to that job immediately. She said you need to apologize to your manager and ask him for your job back! She said, "You moped around this house for 5 months, because you didn't have any money, and all you kept saying is how much you need a job. Just because it gets hard, doesn't mean you quit!" I had to humble myself, swallow my pride and apologize to my manager for my actions. He could have said "no" but he gave me another chance. I learned a valuable lesson on pride and gratefulness that day.

I surprised my mom, on her birthday, and showed her the lyric video for "Sweet Tea on Sundays." She quipped, "I might be biased, but I think this is the best song you ever wrote!" I encourage anyone who's reading this, if your mother is still alive, to give her a big hug and tell her how much you love her! It doesn't matter how busy you are, remember, there is a time for everything, so there is always time for Mama!

CHAPTER 14:
The Art of Storytelling
(Vandrossed)

I have this thing that I do on every album I make. I write at least one song that contains a single extended verse, devoid of a hook or chorus. I usually tell a very descriptive story, purposefully omitting the hook, to allow the listener time to marinate on the story that was just told. If you're familiar with my catalog, you may have caught on to this by now.

Some of my favorite emcees are extraordinary storytellers. Nas, Ice Cube, The Notorious B.I.G., Andre 3000, Slick Rick, Eminem, Scarface and Ghostface Killah all come to mind when I think of the greats. These artists have mastered the art of painting vivid imagery with their words. They draw you in, with their attention to detail, leaving you hanging on the edge of your seat, from bar to bar.

Ice Cube is my absolute favorite. His timing and use of humor and brutal honesty are impeccable. "Jumped back in my lowrider, coming out feeling about 10lbs lighter," Cube raps, after stopping by his mom's house to use the bathroom. His stories are so relatable, and I believe they're a huge reason why he's so successful, as an actor and filmmaker. He seamlessly transitioned from telling stories on wax to telling them on the big screen.

For "Vandrossed," I channeled another one of hip-hop's elite storytellers –- Ghostface Killah. What makes Ghostface so good is not just *what* he says, but *how* he says it. He invokes passion and emotion into every bar, so much so, that you believe these stories really happened, even if it's obvious they're fictional. It's also customary for him to rhyme on top of old school vocal samples, which influenced me to do the same on "Vandrossed."

Like "My Favorite Color," this song was also a result of that 31-Day challenge. In the same manner, I wrote this song, prior to having a beat for it. Unlike "My Favorite Color," though, I knew exactly what I wanted the music to sound like, and I knew just the producer to pull it off.

Up to this point, I hadn't worked with Troy Cedeño on this album. Although he was the sole producer for my previous album, *Frisson*, I wanted to go in a different direction on this project. I like working with multiple producers, because it stretches your creativity. You also develop an understanding of their styles and strengths, which helps you, as the artist, determine who's best equipped to give you exactly what you're looking for. I wanted "Vandrossed" to "sound" like something Ghostface would rap to. I wanted it to feel like a soulful classic. Troy was the only one who could make this record.

What really makes this song special is *how* it was produced. Troy normally produces music, all by himself, as he has proven time and time again that he's more than capable of. Since we've worked so closely over the past seven years, he has learned to trust my "producer" ear. He invited me to be his co-pilot and, together, we built the music around my pre-written verse.

I knew I wanted to rap over a Luther Vandross sample, so that was our beginning point. I needed one of Luther's slower tempo songs, in order to tell the story at a slow pace. I started going through his catalog, and when I listened to "Love Won't Let Me Wait," it was clear that this was the obvious choice.

In true Ghostface fashion, he loves to rap on top of the crooner's vocals, while telling the story, and I wanted to stay true to that. Troy and I found a section of the song, where Luther says, "I need to have you next to me." We looped that line and spaced it out, so it could breathe throughout the track. The idea is to give the listener some ear candy, then briefly take it away, so they can miss it, then bring it back. This is textbook songwriting.

It was imperative to keep the drums very minimal. Kick, rimshot and a little hi-hat, was all it needed. I suggested the rimshot, instead of the traditional snare, because it made the track sound more intimate. This would prove to be one of the best decisions made during the production process. The snare sound would have been too harsh, which could have caused too much of a distraction, and taken away from the story. The rimshot was more R&B sounding, and that's what we were going for. The kick had to have the right pattern, as well. I wanted it to pulsate, but not too much. It didn't need to be too busy. Less was truly more, in this instance.

Troy has a go-to plug-in that he uses, called OPUS. The sound bank he swears by is called "Voices of Soul." Inside this feature, you have voice samples that you can manipulate to sing in whatever key you want them too. You can use it as a solo lead or have them sing as a choir. Troy utilizes this plug-in to perfection. It sounds like we brought in some professional background singers to help Luther out!

I love the bassline that Troy wrote for this song. It has a sexiness to it that is very alluring, and it helps to keep the story intriguing. You'll also find a wineglass-toasting sound effect that occurs once every 8 bars. This was an idea I threw in to give the song a little pizazz.

While it would be convenient to have a fully developed concept in mind before you write, you don't have to wait on one to get started. Sometimes, the subject matter is revealed as you go along. I didn't know where this song was going when I came up with the first few lines. Honestly, I just liked the way the words rolled off my tongue, "Cruisin' through the Bay with my Bae, at a Subaru's pace. As U2 would say, it's a beautiful day." It wasn't until I used a Luther Vandross song title, as a play on words a couple of bars into the song, that I realized where I wanted to go with the song.

As you've probably gathered by now, I love challenging my creativity, so I came up with a brilliant idea. I wondered if I could tell a compelling story, from start to finish, using multiple Luther Vandross song titles as references. There's a line in the song where I state, "My mind is complex, I'm never thinking something simple." I stand on that. I'm wired for complexity, when it comes to this business of rap. I like to be set apart. It's a certain standard I've set for myself, and once you've swam in the deep end, the shallow end just seems boring.

The references had to be strategically placed, in order to push the story forward. The level of difficulty was extremely high, and that excited me!

So, here's the premise: We have a man driving with his woman in a classic car, and they're listening to Luther Vandross. Inspired by the music and the love for his lady, he decides to pull to the side of the road to express his feelings toward her. This ultimately leads to an impromptu marriage proposal. The classic car, a Lincoln Continental, represents the song itself. The music "sounds" like an old classic. When telling your story, the more descriptive you are, the more engaged your listeners will be.

This is not the first time I used a Lincoln Continental to tell a story. The first time was with my group KRK. We wrote a song called "Whitewalls," where the hook goes "Drop top, old school, Lincoln. Whitewalls, rolling with my lady." That song was produced by Troy as well.

I originally wrote "Whitewalls" as a solo song for Theo Lane. I wasn't even planning on rapping on it. I ended up writing an 8-bar rap, but the intent was to showcase my songwriting ability, outside of the hip-hop genre. However, after a while, much like "Grey Gucci Shades," the song started to collect digital dust.

When we formed KRK, we needed some material to work on. I remembered that "Whitewalls" wasn't finished yet. We had Theo's part recorded and my verse was done, too. All we needed was O.G. to write and record his verse and, suddenly, it was a KRK song!

The song came out so great that we decided to shoot a music video for it. There was just one problem, though – we were describing a specific and rare car that none of us owned! After days of vigorously searching, high and low, for someone who owned an old school Lincoln Continental, I found a guy on Instagram, who lived less than 30 miles away.

Jason, also known as "Lincoln Addict," owns a shiny red, '65 Lincoln Continental, that he rents out for weddings and photo shoots. He had never let anyone rent his car for a music video, but he took a chance on us, and it turned out magnificent! We even let Jason have a cameo in the video. You can search it on YouTube under "KRK – Whitewalls" to see us and this vintage, yet vivacious, vehicle in action.

We didn't know it, at the time, but "Whitewalls" would eventually open a huge door for KRK and our producer, Troy Cedeno. I submitted the song to a sync licensing agency. For those who are unfamiliar with this type of company, they help artists get their music placed in Film, TV and Gaming. The company loved our song, so much, that they brought the four of us on, as a songwriting team, after an extensive vetting process. They really enjoyed the vintage sound of "Whitewalls," so they asked if we could submit more songs that represented that '70s era.

We came up with "SOUL SUPPLY," as our songwriting name. This is exactly what I had been hoping and praying for, the opportunity to show that I could write more than just "Rap" and compete on a professional level. We recently landed our first sync placement deal, with not just one, but three songs featured in Season One of Kevin Hart's new adult animated series *Lil Kev,* available now on BET Plus!

"Vandrossed" is kind of like the "unofficial" sequel to "Whitewalls." I didn't set out for it to be, but I realized it one day when I was playing it in my headphones. So, on the same day I recorded "The Florida Room," in an eerily similar impromptu manner to the male character in "Vandrossed," I asked Theo to reiterate a part of the "Whitewalls" chorus, for the song's outro. "Rollin' with my lady, rollin' with my girl!" I won't charge you anything for that little easter egg!

I'm so glad I remained open to working with Troy again, for this album, even though I was searching for production from new producers. He and I have developed a chemistry that I absolutely love tapping into. He makes it so easy to write incredible songs and to tell compelling stories, due to his years of expertise as a dope producer. Whether it's KRK, SOUL SUPPLY or Shadcore, I know it's going to be just like that Lincoln Continental – a straight up classic!

CHAPTER 15:
Hold On, Honey Bake
(En Vogue)

Not again??? It happened not once, but twice. Remember earlier when I talked about the time I thought the album was complete, and I ended up writing an additional song, "The Florida Room"? Well, the same thing happened with "En Vogue." I was convinced that the album was truly done this time. Not only was I done with the album, but my book was written, typed and completely edited. The audiobook was fully recorded and in the post-production phase. I wasn't even actively writing any new material, purposely, because I didn't want this very thing to happen. Besides, I was literally a couple months away from both the book and the album being released, so there was no way anything new was going to be added at that point. Or so, I thought.

It all began with a conversation I had with my daughter, Kailey. I don't know how we got on the subject, but we were talking about the time I won a trip to New York in the *VH-1 Freestyle59 Competition*. Kailey was just a baby at the time, so now as an adult, she was interested in hearing me retell the story, and she wanted a play-by-play recap of the whole experience.

I told her how my limo driver was waiting for me, holding a sign that read "Mr. Rashad Harrell." Kailey's eyes lit up and she said, "Wow, that's so cool!" I told her about the conversation the driver and I had on the way to the hotel. He shared the fact that he chauffeured a laundry list of big name rap artists around in the past; how some were super cool and others, not so much. I told her about the historic Algonquin Hotel I stayed at in Manhattan. This prompted me to get on the laptop to "google" the Algonquin Hotel so I could show her pictures of this most elegant establishment. Going down memory lane was a special moment I was able to share with my youngest child.

The next morning, I was lying in my bed and staring at the ceiling at 5:30A.M. Our conversation replayed in my head, as I thought to myself just how close I was to seeing my dream come into full fruition during that time in my life. This was a competition where the grand prize winner would come home $10,000 dollars richer and have the opportunity to have a face-to-face with two major record label executives. I came in 2nd place and ultimately went home empty-handed.

As I was lying on the mattress, thinking about the stories I shared with Kailey the night before, the first four lines just seemed to appear out of thin air: *It's so bizarre thinking about my "Close, but no cigars." Wrote some of the dopest bars, hoping to be a global star. Chauffeur drove the car from LaGuardia to the Algonquin. I'm in the backseat like, "Is this a malfunction?"*

The conversation I had with my daughter made me relive key moments from that New York visit, so much so that I was able to reconnect with certain specific feelings I felt, even on the ride from the airport to the hotel. I remember thinking, "This can't really be happening right now." I'm in the mecca of Hip-Hop, riding in this luxurious Lincoln Continental, looking at these gargantuan skyscrapers, all because I spat a fifty-nine second freestyle. In a couple of days, four other rappers and I are going to head over to VH-1 studios to record videos that will be shown all over the world. This is what I've always dreamed of and it is finally happening, for real!

Those 4 lines I came up with quickly turned into 12. By noon, I had 24 lines. I couldn't stop. The rhymes kept coming, so I kept writing. These reflections I was having continued to inspire more and more compelling lyrics, and there was so much freedom in expressing these thoughts and memories, first in my head and then transferred to my phone. At the end of my shift, I had a whopping 42-bar verse! No hook, just one long verse of pure passion and raw emotion. Anyone who has ever felt so close to achieving something they want so badly, and, for them, giving up is not an option, can relate to this particular verse. I still didn't have a beat to spit it to, but more importantly, I didn't have any real intentions of recording a new song in the first place, much less adding it to my album. "Stick to your guns. Stick to the plan, Shad. No more songs. The album is done," I surmised. This verse *is* special, though. OK, so maybe I'll see if I have some beats available from my Ukraine connection, and if I do decide to record it, I'll release it as a one-off. I will under no circumstances add it to *I Left a Mess in There*. Sounds like a plan.

I love how God orders our steps, whether we're aware of it or not. I go to my email to search for the latest beat packs from the Ukrainian producer Svgar. The second track I listened to immediately grabbed my attention. I started spittin' the verse to the track: *It's so bizarre thinking about my "Close, but no cigars." Wrote some of the dopest bars, hoping to be a global star.* Oh my goodness! This is the perfect beat for this song! It's almost as if I wrote the rap to the beat and not the other way around. This is the type of music that you reflect and bare your soul on. The way I rode the beat and how it complemented what I was saying was undeniable. "Wait a minute. Let me make sure no one has already copped this beat before I get too excited," I thought. So, I quickly sent my guy an email to confirm that the beat was still available for purchase. "Yes, it's still available," he responded. Awesome news! It must be meant to be.

Something just dawned on me as I'm writing this—something I hadn't even considered before. Producers often name their tracks, which helps to better organize them. I usually don't pay too much attention to what the producer named the track because I always rename it to whatever title I come up with, but I noticed he named this one "Sanctum." I looked up the definition of this word, and it means "A sacred or holy place where one is free from intrusion." This can refer to the inner chamber of a temple, church, or other place of worship. Wow! This makes so much sense, now that I think about it! What I am sharing on this song is an invitation for the listener to enter a sacred place, a chamber of mine that is normally reserved for only a chosen few. That explains why the music and what I'm saying fits together like a hand in glove. Talk about God ordering your steps.

Ok, let's get back to the story. Once I realized that the track was still available, I went and recorded a scratch demo on my phone. Like I do with many of my demos, I shared it through Messenger with a few of my friends and fellow rap peers. I like to get their reactions and this is a way we continue to inspire each other. Some of them responded with fire emojis. Others said things like, "Super dope, Shad!" or "Wild as a clouded leopard in the Malaysian jungle!?!" However, one response in particular, had me picking my jaw up off the floor.

Before I share that reaction, let me give you the vision I had as I was writing this song. I imagined my 2-year-old granddaughter sitting on my lap the whole time, as if I were performing these lyrics for her. You know the expression, "This is a story I can tell my grandkids one day." Well, this is my version of telling my granddaughter a cool story, but in rhyme form, while sitting in a rocking chair with her on my lap. Keep that image in mind as I share my homie Bongo's reaction to the demo I sent.

"Front porch, food on the grill, grandbaby on the lap." Are you kidding me? This is the epitome of great minds thinking alike! I couldn't believe how we pretty much saw the same thing. I told him how I had the same imagery of my granddaughter sitting on my lap, if I were ever to shoot a music video for this song. He then responded, "The visuals are already there. This is not desperation. It's like a chill confidence that comes from wisdom." Such an encouraging response from a fellow emcee, who I highly revere, is not one to simply gloss over. I took into account all of these different reactions, and suddenly there became this urgency to officially record the song.

I was due to go to the studio in less than a week, anyway, to record a theme song for the school that I work at, so I figured I could kill two birds with one stone by knocking out this new song while I was there. On the day of my appointment, an interesting idea came to mind. Since I had already pictured myself rapping the lyrics to my granddaughter, Athens, why not record her voice on my phone, so I could include it on the actual song?

Before I left for the studio, I said, "Come here, Honey Bake." I nicknamed her "Honey Bake" when she was just a few days old because her fat little cheeks reminded me of a honey baked ham. I know, ridiculous right? Well, too bad. She's my Honey Bake and that's all there is to it. When I called her over, I asked her to say, "I love you, Pop-Pop!" She said that and a little more. I knew right then that this song was going to be special.

As I was wrapping up my session, the next clients were entering the room. In walks a guy who I've been knowing for close to 30 years. His name is Esto and I hadn't seen him in well over 20 years. Esto was part of a rap group back in the 90s known as "The Archives." Their producer, Rook, would later go on to help form the Grammy Award-winning production team known as Justice League, the group responsible for some of music's biggest hits from artists like Lil' Wayne, Rick Ross, Jeezy and Mary J. Blige, to name a few.

We chopped it up about old times when we used to rhyme in ciphers together, and he introduced me to his 22-year-old son, Taj, who is also an artist, and Taj's friend. Before I left, I asked the engineer, James, to let Esto hear what we had just worked on since I knew he hadn't heard me rap in years. He couldn't stop shaking his head and the expression on his face said it all: "Shad, you still got it!"

His son's friend chimed in, "You slid on that, O.G.!" I told him I appreciated the compliment, especially coming from a young cat like himself. He said, "Real talk, some people just be trying too hard, but you can tell that you know what you talkin' 'bout." He also said the song has replay value. His words reminded me of Bongo's when he said that there was a "chill confidence that comes from wisdom" when he heard the scratch demo. Now here were two very similar takes from two guys who have at least 20 years in between them. That fact was not easily lost on me.

It's worth mentioning that I didn't name this song until I was finished recording it. I usually don't operate like that, but I knew the title would eventually reveal itself. As I've stated before, I like to really put some thought into what I name my songs. I started thinking about the main idea of the song. Sometimes, the title is a word or a phrase that was mentioned in the actual song, so I began looking at the lyrics on my phone. I liked the line where I said, "So when I finally get it, I'll hold on to it tighter than En Vogue," referring to the moment my dream comes into full fruition. For those of you who don't know, En Vogue was a popular female R&B group in the 90s, and their debut single was called "Hold On". Well, "holding on" seems to be the main idea of what I'm trying to convey, but there's no way I'm going to title it "Hold On." That's too basic and it's already overused. If I call it "En Vogue," it requires you to take an extra thought to make the correlation. I'm essentially telling my granddaughter, and whoever else is within earshot of my voice, to hang in there. Hold on. You never know how close you are to your breakthrough moment. Quitting and giving up is not an option.

So, how did the song end up on the album? I'm glad you asked. When I came home from the studio, I couldn't wait to show Honey Bake. I wanted to see her reaction to hearing her own voice on a song for the first time. She was out with her mom and her Aunt, so I let my wife hear it and she loved it. She asked if I was going to put it on my album. I told her I didn't plan on adding it, and that it felt like it should have its own space, separate from the album.

A few minutes later my granddaughter arrived. When I first played it for her, she was clearly too overstimulated to notice. She kept running around the house and bouncing off the walls. I played it again, and this time I skipped straight to her part. I said, "Honey Bake, listen." This time she sat up straight and her eyes widened. I could see that she recognized her voice coming through the speaker. She started dancing in the living room. Everyone was enjoying her reaction.

I eventually went about my night, opening up my laptop to work on a few things. Honey Bake made her way over to my area, holding the bluetooth speaker we had just played the song on. She said, "I love you, Pop-Pop," a couple times, and I responded, "I love you, too, Honey Bake!" I didn't think much of it, but my wife noticed what was happening. She said, "She wants you to play the song again!" I didn't realize it, but my wife was absolutely right! Remember she said "I love you, Pop-Pop" on the song, so she was trying to get me to run it back!

When her part came around this time, I asked her, "Who is that?" Excitedly, my grandbaby said, "Athens. It's Athens!" Honey Bake's excitement and enthusiasm is what let me know that *this* song belonged on *this* album. *I Left a Mess in There* is all about "making an impact" and "leaving your footprint". Establishing a legacy. What better way to capture that than by showcasing this special song that features my granddaughter on this particular body of work?

There is a deeper reason I named this song "En Vogue." It deals with the actual definition of the term. "En Vogue" means "in current fashion or style." This piece is a reminder that songs with substance and weight will always be in style. Gimmicks come and go. Fads are fleeting. The "real", however, will always remain relevant. Love for family is always current. Being vulnerable enough to let the listener into your sanctum should always be "trending" and being a dope emcee never gets old. Remain authentic. Remain yourself and you will always be en vogue.

CHAPTER 16:
Leave A Mess
(Do Something Dope Today)

I t's so cliché to say, "I saved the best for last", but when it comes to the final song on *I Left a Mess in There,* that's precisely what I did! I knew when I recorded "Do Something Dope Today," that it would close out the album. Even though it was probably the fourth or fifth song I wrote and recorded for the project, it just felt like a perfect final thought to leave the listener with. This song summarizes the entire album.

"Leaving a mess" means to leave an impact, or dare I say a footprint, for whoever you're fortunate enough to come in contact with. We were born to be atmosphere-shifters! There should be something different in the air, when you exit the room. These truths were the driving force behind the creation of this album. Every lyric and bar on every song had to tie back to the title *I Left a Mess in There.*

But how does one leave a mess? It starts and ends with "doing something dope today." I got up this morning and went to the gym for an hour. I was doing something dope by working out, to improve my physical *and* mental health. Before I went to the gym, I prayed, then I read Galatians 5:13-26. I was doing something dope by spending time with God, learning His ways, in order to improve my spiritual health. As I'm writing this, I'm at the library with my daughter, Kailey. I brought her along to see her dad go after his dream of writing a potentially life-changing book, in hopes that she'll be inspired to go after her own dreams. That's doing something dope.

The act of doing something dope will look like different things for different people. It all boils down to one thing, really –

being your best self. For one person, that could mean enrolling in school to further their education. For another it could also mean not purchasing that pack of cigarettes. Find your "dope" thing and decide to do it, today.

My head is always full of wonderful ideas, but I also tend to procrastinate, and not act on many of them. I found out a hard truth around 20 years ago. It had been prophesied by a young pastor that my wife and I possessed witty ideas and witty inventions. Shortly after that encounter, we started having brainstorming sessions to come up with ideas for new inventions. One of my ideas, (which to my knowledge did not exist at the time), was Hallmark cards that played music when you open them. I imagined the reader, hearing my voice, as I rapped the words that were printed on the inside of the card. My wife agreed that this was a genius idea.

Here's the hard truth that I learned: If you do not act on an idea that God gives you, He surely will pass that idea along to someone who will. Even though I felt like this was a unique invention, ultimately, I didn't pursue it and I talked myself out of trying. I didn't know the first place to start. I convinced myself that it would be too difficult to pull off without the proper resources. I came up with every excuse in the book of why it wouldn't work, instead of asking God to help bring my vision into fruition. Nowadays, these types of cards can be found all over the world. Someone else chose to "do something dope" and made the idea in their head a reality.

I share this story because, unfortunately, I'm not alone when it comes to making excuses for why something won't work out. We're all guilty. Why do we do that? Is it fear? What if I fail? So, what! At least you tried. Here's a better question. What if I *succeed?* What if it works out? Or better yet, why *not* me?

I came up with the saying, "do something dope today" about 6 years ago. I was hoping to create a cool and catchy phrase, to keep myself motivated and far away from procrastination. I wasn't happy with that version of me. As a creative, you can often find yourself in a "funk," if you're not actively creating something new and exciting. I needed a personal reminder that life is short, and if I was going to do anything meaningful, during my existence, it should be done sooner than later. "Why put off until tomorrow what could be done today?" was my mentality.

When I was trying to come up with my own slogan, I wanted it to have a "hip-hop feel" to it, to keep it true to who I am. It all seemed to come together in an instant – "Do Something Dope Today!" It had a nice ring to it, so I started saying it around friends and family members. I even began to use it as a hashtag on some of my social media posts. Next, I started printing it on T-shirts, caps and more. When Covid first hit, I had masks made with "Do Something Dope Today" plastered on the front. It wasn't until I started working on this album that I decided to turn the slogan into a song.

When I first heard the instrumental from Svgar Beats, I said, "Oh, he's just showing out, now!" It had this energy to it that drew me in. I couldn't just hop on this beat and talk about anything that lacked substance. This beat was a serious attention-grabber, so the subject matter had to provide the same intensity.

Up to this point, I had never rapped over a "drill" beat, but I was confident I could convincingly pull it off. Drill Music is usually performed by younger artists, who rap very aggressively, with dark lyrics as the theme. The snare drum patterns are typically busy, with a heavy dose of 808s to accompany them. It's like Trap Music, but with a bit of a twist. Although the subject matter of most Drill Music isn't my cup of tea, I do find the instrumentation and the musicality to be quite intriguing. Whenever I work on a new project, I look to do something that I've never done, so this energetic beat was exactly what I needed to put a new feather in my rap cap.

Originally, I thought about using the beat for KRK, but Theo and O.G. thought it was better suited as a solo Shadcore song. I said "cool" and I started thinking about what I could talk about over this track, and how it would fit into the flow of the album. I remembered I wanted to turn my new slogan, "Do Something Dope Today" into a song, so I began to spit that phrase over the beat. It felt good in my soul, so I tweaked and polished it until it had a nice, sparkling finish!

I wanted to feature someone who held similar values and ideals as my own. I could have done the song by myself, but I wanted to share space with a fellow emcee, who would be able to match my ferocity and passion. For me, the obvious choice was Charli Funk. Being familiar with his work and his rapid-fire delivery, I knew that he was more than capable of locking in and taking this song to a whole new level. It made sense to include my brother, since he's all about positivity plus he's a "dope" emcee!

Like I do with all my co-collaborators, I sent him a voice memo, explaining the direction for the song, along with a scratch recording of my verse. He responded with a "Wow" emoji, and a day later he sent his verse. It was exactly what I expected from him -- pure lava! He rode the beat like his life depended on it.

Many artists would shy away from working with someone who they consider to be just as good, if not better, than they are. They fear the possibility of being outshone. I feel the opposite. I want super talented people on my songs, because that will inevitably bring out the best in me. The minute I decided I was going to feature Charli on this song, I knew I had to go to a different place, lyrically. Having this type of mindset will only help improve your artistry.

Here is what I also know. Charli Funk is aware of what I'm capable of, too. So, guess what? He's doing the same thing on his end. He's going into an elevated level of thinking for his verse. We're purposefully seeking to bring out the best in each other. This will only make the song come out that much better. We both lit the vocal booth up that night and left a huge mess in there!

On a side note, in 2025 Charli Funk and I decided to work on a full project together. We go by the name "It's 7:27 Somewhere," which is an ode to our hometown, St. Petersburg, FL. Troy Cedeño was so excited at the idea of the two of us releasing an entire project together that he asked if he could produce every track for us! It was an obvious "yes" from Charli and I. Our debut single "Burg Energy" is now currently available on all major streaming platforms.

The intro to "Do Something Dope Today" was empty at first, so the mixing engineer, James Wood, suggested that Charli Funk or I give the urban dictionary definition of the word "dope" at the beginning. I love the clarity of Charli's voice, so I asked him to do the honors. He was excited at the opportunity, as he shared that he wanted to get into doing voiceover work anyways. He knocked it out in just two takes.

The day after we recorded the song, I was scheduled to do a rap presentation at an elementary school for the Great American Teach-In. This was another opportunity to do something "dope" that day. I used to do these presentations quite often, when my children were in elementary school. I was grateful that I was being requested all these years later by a different school. I gave the students a brief history of hip-hop music and culture. One of the exercises in my presentation included me writing a word on the board and asking the students to participate by coming up with as many rhyming words as they could for the original word. Later, I put on an instrumental and I did a "freestyle" rap, using all the words that were listed on the board. For my final move, I performed "Do Something Dope Today."

Believe me when I tell you, those students lost their minds, completely! They all got up off the floor and started dancing, with some doing moves I had never seen before. It was such an adrenaline rush for me. I left feeling rather victorious. Here I was, in my late forties, making music that made 10- and 12-year-olds dance their little hearts out.

Four months later, I was invited back to the school to perform for their Black History Month celebration. By then, I had recorded some new music, so I performed my song, "Locs." One student, who had a headful of dreadlocks, came on stage with me and started shaking his dreads, non-stop. His classmates cheered him on, so he continued until he got dizzy! The energy I received from the 3rd through 5th graders was incredible!

What happened next was the kicker. I had a few minutes remaining before my time was up, so I asked the kids if I should do another song. One little girl yelled out, "Do 'Do Something Dope Today'!" I couldn't believe she remembered the title of the song. Of course, I gave the students what they were looking for, and we ended on another high note.

We often make the mistake of thinking we have more "time." We tell ourselves "I'll start tomorrow." How many times have we repeatedly said those words over and again? How many ideas are held captive in our heads, begging for a release date? What if *your* idea is the key to someone else's breakthrough? The first word in "Do Something Dope Today" is an action word. "Do" means perform. Make it happen.

I decided I would do something "dope" when I made this album, but it didn't stop there. God said, "This isn't just a regular album." He told me, "Son, for this album, I want you to write an entire book about it. Don't worry about if it's going to sell or who's going to read it. Just be obedient and I'll handle the rest."

I hope you found some inspiration within these pages. I am just a vessel. I give God all the glory, honor and praise for any motivation these words may have provided and for any fires that were lit under your bottoms. Hit me up at shadcore92@gmail.com I'd love to hear your feedback. I'll leave you with this fact: You can't spell "message" without leaving a "mess." Peace.

ACKNOWLEDGEMENTS

This is actually the hardest part of a book to write, in my opinion. How do you quantify in so many words what roles certain people played in motivating you to complete such a big idea? Then what if you leave someone out? Once it's in print, you can't take it back. Well, like Diana Nyad, sometimes you have to just dive in, so here goes!

I want to start by thanking God. Without His guidance and the Holy Spirit nudging me to do something "special" on this go around, you would not be reading this right now. I was obedient to the call and I believe He will honor that obedience, however He sees fit. His love is eternal and perfect in every way.

Thank you to the love of my life. My beautiful, loving wife, Tonya Harrell. I would not want to take this journey with anyone else in the world. You are my best friend and I thank you for always being in my corner. We get each other and I'm grateful because not everyone is able to say or have that. Twenty-seven years and counting! Let's continue this divine covenant thang, my Suga!

To my amazing children, Jaire, Tasanee and Kailey. I love you so much! I am so proud of the incredible adults you've all grown to be. Jaire, you are a wonderful husband, father, son, nephew, grandson, and most importantly, man of God. What a joy it is to have a son, especially one as talented and special as you! Tasanee, I am constantly blown away by your creativity and your ability to excel at whatever you put your mind to. God has something special in store for you. Keep your trust in Him. Kailey, you are my sidekick. You are so daggone smart that it's borderline scary at times! Lol! I love your smile and your sense of humor. Your future is as bright as your yellow punch buggy!

Thank you to my daughter-in-love, Alyana. I love the way you love my son and how you help keep him balanced. What a mighty young woman of God you are! You have been such a delightful addition to our family and I am proud to be your Father-in-law.

To my precious granddaughter, Athens. Pop-Pop is so crazy about you! I can't wait to read this book to you, my sweet, sweet Honey-Bake! You have such an incredible life ahead of you and I'm just grateful I get to be a part of it as your grandfather.

To my mother. Ma, what can I say? I thank you for always believing in me and being my biggest cheerleader! You embody what it means to be a mother. You show up all the time, every time and I'm so proud to be your son. It's because of you that I even have the confidence to write a book in the first place. I love you, my lil' sweet-tea-maker!

To my sisters, April and Autumn. April, you always keep me laughing, not to mention you are one of the most remarkable mothers I know! My nephew could not have asked for a better mom. Auntie Darlene spoke prophecy over you when she nicknamed you "April Sweet". It's a joy to be your big brother, even though you probably think you should've been the oldest! Lol!!! Autumn, ever since you were born I've always liked to kiss your cheeks! Lol! Ok, that might have been a weird way to start this acknowledgement, but I just love greeting you that way because you are my baby sister and I feel protective over you. What an amazing job you did editing my book! It would not be nearly as good as it is without your help. You are such an amazing woman, with too many skills to name. I am so glad to be your big brother. I got some dope siblings y'all!

To my father, Larry D. Legend (allegedly). Even though you are no longer here physically, you were very much with me during the making of this album and the writing of this book. I love the example you set for me as a husband and as a father. I can't thank you enough for being my real life superhero. You left an undeniable mess in there! I miss you so much, Pops. I hope I made you proud.

To everyone who contributed on the album to make it the masterpiece that it is, I thank you from the bottom of my heart. J. Ack, you are not only an incredible emcee but you are the true definition of a friend. Always available to help assist with my creative ideas and always down to hop on a track and "eat everything" with me! Forever the Sam to my Denzel.

Give Gen a hug and a kiss for me. Love you, bro! Troy Cedeño, we are attached at the hip, buddy. You ain't never going nowhere and neither am I! Thanks for the incredible production and, more importantly, for the friendship. I enjoy getting to sit in the cockpit as your co-pilot! O.G., my lil' big brother! Lol! I am so proud of you homie.

You are one of the realest dudes I know. Your passion inspires me to keep going. The only guy I know who works harder than I do in that studio! Thanks for your contribution to the album, homie. Theo, my soul brother! I'm so glad we connected back in 2016.

It's been nothing but up ever since! Let's keep it going. You are a straight up beast with those vocals! I love the brotherhood that you, O.G. and myself have created together as KRK and as SOUL SUPPLY, with Cedeño! Shout out to your lovely wives, Juli, April and Meechie! We are officially family and that's a beautiful thing! Eliana, you continue to amaze me! The best vocalist in all of Tampa Bay, and I will forever shout that from the mountaintop! You added the right amount of "honey" to the album, as you always do! We make an incredible team, don't you think? Lol! Charli Funk, it's 7:27 somewhere, my G! You never disappoint! NEVER! Flow of the century and you're so humble about it. Keep shining, young king! To all the producers who were a part of the album, to my mixing engineer, James Wood (you're an absolute beast) and to my mastering engineer, Dave Greenberg (so glad to have your hands bless this project), I want to say thank you!

To my homie, Justin Finity! Thank you for reigniting the spark by asking me to guest feature on "Carnage". You brought the energy I needed to start the album out. I just thought about something; "Carnage" is basically the same thing as "Leaving a Mess in There!" Lol! Thank you to my brother, Marlon McCaulsky, not only for the book design and typesetting, but for always being willing to help me in this authorial landscape. I tell you all the time that you inspired me to write books in the first place! I appreciate you, homie. To the legend himself, Big Rube.

This makes our third collaboration together, and this one probably means the most. Your words and that iconic voice continue to reverberate throughout the annals of Hip-Hop culture. We are better off for your presence in this genre we love so much. Thank you for the kind words, and for setting the book in motion.

Lastly, I want to thank all of my colleagues, my family, friends, Victory Christian Center Church family, professors, mentors, acquaintances and the readers of this book. I thank you for investing your time and your efforts into my passion. I do not take it for granted. Until next time, one love.

by RASHAD "SHADCORE" HARRELL

Get the album, I Left A Mess In There, at

www.shadcore.com